The Frolicks
or The Lawyer Cheated
(1671)

THE FROLICKS

or *The Lawyer Cheated*

(1671)

▼

ELIZABETH POLWHELE

EDITED FROM THE MANUSCRIPT IN THE
CORNELL UNIVERSITY LIBRARIES
BY JUDITH MILHOUS
AND ROBERT D. HUME

CORNELL UNIVERSITY PRESS

ITHACA AND LONDON

This book has been published with the aid of grants from the Hull Memorial Publication Fund of Cornell University and from the Andrew W. Mellon Foundation.

First published 1977 by Cornell University Press.
Published in the United Kingdom by Cornell University Press Ltd., 2–4 Brook Street, London W1Y 1AA.

International Standard Book Number 0-8014-1030-4
Library of Congress Catalog Card Number 77-3125
Printed in the United States of America by Vail-Ballou Press, Inc.
Librarians: Library of Congress cataloging information appears on the last page of the book.

For Blot, an effishent mews

PREFACE

The name Elizabeth Polwhele is unfamiliar even to specialists in Restoration drama. Polwhele was, like Aphra Behn, among the first women to write for the professional theatre in England, although neither of her two plays was ever published. Until recently, *The Faithful Virgins* was known only as an anonymous and undated manuscript in the Bodleian Library, while *The Frolicks* was considered "lost." The rediscovery of *The Frolicks,* and the consequent attribution of *The Faithful Virgins* to Polwhele, has created almost ex nihilo a "new" Restoration playwright, and a most interesting one.

The Frolicks is here published for the first time. Although known to scholars in the nineteenth century, the manuscript of the play disappeared toward the end of the century; it turns out to have been purchased sometime after 1890 by the attorney and book collector Benno Loewy (1854–1919), who bequeathed it to Cornell University. It was catalogued in 1924 and has remained at Cornell ever since. Moving some books in the basement of the library in the spring of 1974, Donald D. Eddy of the Department of Rare Books noticed a seventeenth-century play and brought it to our attention. Author and title were enough to tell us that this was a "lost" play of some significance, but we had no idea that Polwhele had written it to be produced professionally or that her earlier play had almost certainly been mounted by the Duke's Company.

The Frolicks was written at a particularly interesting point in the development of Restoration drama, when the chaste and moral comedies that predominated in the 1660s began to give way to the sex comedies which were to flood the theatres in the middle 1670s. Like the first plays of William Congreve and George Farquhar in the years to come, *The Frolicks* (1671) is a lively, imitative work that reflects the theatrical circumstances from which it springs. Polwhele knew what was going on in the London theatre, and she made her play au courant. There is no record of its performance, but clearly the author wrote it with production in mind. It is an enjoyable—and spicy—example of Restoration comedy, and its raciness comes at a surprisingly early date. Aphra Behn was not to write a play like this one for another six years. Whoever Elizabeth Polwhele may have been—the biographical problems are fascinating but frustrating—she was an ambitious and observant young writer, and in *The Frolicks* she succeeded in turning out a brisk romantic farce that remains as stageworthy as most of its contemporaries.

We have designed this edition with our readers' convenience foremost in mind. What was written to entertain should not be weighted down by ponderous scholarly apparatus and archaic spelling. We have thus followed a policy of modernization and regularization, "along consciously conservative lines," as John Loftis writes of the Regents Restoration Drama Series. The result, we hope, leaves the reader free to respond to the gaiety of the play itself.

We are indebted to Donald D. Eddy and to the Library Board of the Cornell University Libraries for permission to publish this edition of Cornell MSS. Bd. Rare P P77.

To Harold F. Brooks, Donald D. Eddy, Kathryn Hume, Shirley Strum Kenny, Edward A. Langhans, Arthur H. Scouten, Irène Simon, and Colin Visser we are grateful for advice, criticism, and information. For bibliographical help we owe thanks to Laetitia Yeandle of the Folger Shakespeare Library. For assistance with problems in English law we are indebted to Richard Weisberg of Cleary, Gottlieb, Steen, and Hamilton, and of Columbia University.

We are grateful to the staffs of the Newberry, Folger, and Houghton libraries for expert assistance. The librarian of Dr. Williams's Library (London) was most gracious in answering inquiries. We owe particular thanks to Robert Nikirk of the Grolier Club and to Edwin E. Williams of Harvard University.

A brief preliminary account of Elizabeth Polwhele and her plays appeared in *Papers of the Bibliographical Society of America*, 71 (1977). We thank the editor for allowing us to use some of our material from that note.

J.M. and R.D.H.

University of Iowa
Cornell University

CONTENTS

ILLUSTRATIONS

INTRODUCTION
A "LOST" PLAY AND ITS CONTEXT

English drama was in a state of flux around 1670. Every writer tried to gauge audience taste, hoping to find the formula which would produce a hit. *The Frolicks* is particularly interesting for its skillful anticipation of some future trends in comedy. Polwhele was either very lucky or a shrewd judge of changing taste.

The Theatrical Situation circa 1670

In the decade which followed the reopening of the theatres in 1660 both the King's Company and the Duke's Company had flourished, staging large numbers of new plays after 1662, many of them by unknown writers. Yet the aspiring young dramatist could be pardoned some puzzlement about what sort of play to try his hand at. No clear trend had emerged from the multitude of new works. Small as it was, the audience had proved fickle. At this time six days was a decent run: after that a play had to draw many repeat attenders to keep the house passably full. One- and two-day revivals of stock plays—many of them pre-Restoration favorites—were the companies' staple fare, interspersed with new shows which were financially a gamble but which offered the possibility of a bigger return.

Contrary to a hardy myth, "Restoration comedy" is far from monolithic.[1] In the years just before 1670 one might point to Sir George Etherege's *She wou'd if she cou'd* (1668) as an ex-

---

[1] For a fuller account of comedy in these years, the reader can consult Robert D. Hume, *The Development of English Drama in the Late Seventeenth Century* (Oxford: Clarendon Press, 1976).

ample of the quintessential drawing-room "comedy of wit and manners" often associated with the Restoration. But that refined and graceful play had not achieved much success in the theatre—"a silly, dull thing . . . mighty insipid," grumbled Samuel Pepys.[2] By far the largest group of comedies in these years consists of farcical adaptations, many of them from Molière. John Lacy's *Sauny the Scot* (1667) is a crude vulgarization of Shakespeare's *Taming of the Shrew*, while his *Dumb Lady* (acted by 1670) is a coarse but boisterously amusing recension of *Le Médecin malgré lui*. Putting "cow-itch" down someone's back is not the stuff of drawing-room comedy. But as Lacy once observed in a prologue, he wrote his plays "To you that laugh aloud with wide-mouth'd grace, / To see *Jack Pudding*'s Custard thrown in's face." Matthew Medbourne's feeble *Tartuffe*, Richard Flecknoe's wretched *Damoiselles a la Mode*, and John Caryll's lively if trivial *Sir Salomon* are all part of the flood of "French" farce which was sweeping the stage.

Not everyone approved of such vulgarizations. In prefaces and prologues John Dryden excoriates them, bewailing the state of English comedy and championing an alternative—an elevated, upper-class comedy reminiscent of Corneille's concept of *comédie heroïque*. In *Secret-Love* (1667) and *Marriage A-la-Mode* (1671) he had fair success in this genre. His like-minded brother-in-law Edward Howard was less lucky with *The Womens Conquest* (1670) and *The Six days Adventure* (1671), both failures. Thomas Shadwell was loudly proclaiming Ben Jonson as the proper model for Restoration writers; Dryden wanted something more refined and courtly—John Fletcher in "modern" language was closer to his ideal. What the audience would buy remained to be seen.

The bawdiness of Restoration comedy is a popular byword, though Thomas Babington Macaulay's picture of a pack of debauched courtiers drooling over smut has long been discre-

---

[2] *Diary*, 6 February 1668. All quotations are from *The Diary of Samuel Pepys*, ed. Robert Latham and William Matthews, 11 vols. (London: Bell, 1970—   ).

dited. Even specialists do not always seem to realize just how much the sex comedy we associate with the period is a phenomenon of the 1670s and later. William Wycherley's *Country-Wife* (1675), Etherege's *Man of Mode* (1676), Thomas Durfey's *Fond Husband* (1677), Dryden's notorious and little-read *Mr. Limberham* (1678), and Edward Ravenscroft's *London Cuckolds* (1681) would have been quite unthinkable in the 1660s. During the 1670s there is a steady escalation in sex and titillation as dramatists exploit shock value ever further. The boom is analogous to developments in the New York theatre during the 1960s: the shows exhibiting full frontal nudity late in the decade would not have attracted a middleclass audience ten years earlier, even had the police allowed them to remain open.

As late as 1667 the times were by no means ripe for as moderately gamey a play as Fletcher's and Massinger's *Custom of the Country* (1620). Richard Legh reported that the audience found the play "so damn'd bawdy that the Ladyes flung their peares and fruites at the Actors." Pepys— no puritan—found the show completely unattractive, and others must have shared his opinion, for at the only other performance of which we have record, he found "the house mighty empty—more than ever I saw it." [3] We tend to forget that the smash hit of the early 1660s was Sir Samuel Tuke's ultrapure, utterly chaste *Adventures of Five Hours* (1663). Cuckolding actions and smutty talk are decidedly not a feature of early Restoration comedy. Thomas Killigrew's *Parsons Wedding* (1641, revived in 1664) is about as racy a play as we will find prior to 1670—a work Pepys dismissed as "loose" and "bawdy." The Dryden-Davenant adaptation of Shakespeare's *Tempest* (1667) and Etherege's *She wou'd if she cou'd* contain discreet hints of titillation, but not until Thomas Betterton's *Amorous Widow* (acted by late 1670) do we find a work in which a cuckolding action really looms

[3] *The London Stage 1660–1800*, pt. 1: 1660–1700, ed. William Van Lennep, Emmett L. Avery, and Arthur H. Scouten (Carbondale: Southern Illinois University Press, 1965), p. 100. Pepys, 2 January and 1 August 1667.

large, and even there it comes to naught. That sex and
bawdry would become the staple devices of seventies comedy
could not readily have been predicted in 1670.

One of the most significant developments of the 1660s,
and one conducive to sex comedy, was the rise of the "gay
couple." [4] The use of a witty couple, railing against marriage
but succumbing to love, is an old device—Shakespeare's Be-
atrice and Benedick in *Much Ado about Nothing* are an obvious example. In this period the duel of wit gets turned into a
basic structural device, and the resulting love game becomes
a major feature of a great many plays. At first young widows
take the female part, as in James Howard's *English Mounsieur* (1663) and Etherege's *Comical Revenge* (1664). But
then Howard dropped the convention of widowhood in *All
Mistaken* (1665), and Dryden followed suit in *Secret-Love*. Of
course much of the point to the love game lies in the taming
of the gallant—and the "wilder" he is, the greater the
woman's triumph. Thus in Etherege's *Man of Mode,* Dorimant (a reflection of the celebrated Earl of Rochester) is a
great womanizer, a rake who enjoys his conquests, but he finally meets his match in Harriet, a woman tough, resource-
ful, and self-disciplined enough to tame him.

Naturally dramatists work their protagonists' libertinism
for what thrill value it is worth. Etherege's glamorous, repre-
hensible Dorimant, Wycherley's insatiable Horner, Dryden's
goatish Woodall—all are meant to fascinate, but also to
shock. Oftener than not, the dashing rake is broke, and his
past is catching up with him. James Howard's Philidor (pursued by indignant women demanding support for his bastards) and Congreve's Valentine thirty years later (grumbling
"a thoughtless . . . Whore, she . . . might have overlaid the
Child a Fortnight ago") are representatives of a numerous
tribe of rakish young spendthrifts in urgent need of a wealthy
wife. But the morality of rewarding a libertine was a problem.
Late in the century tearful "reform" starts to become a common pattern: the dashing young man swears constancy and

[4] See John Harrington Smith, *The Gay Couple in Restoration Comedy*
(Cambridge, Mass.: Harvard University Press, 1948).

virtue on his knees, and we are ponderously assured that he will change his tomcat ways. Even early in the period there was a good deal of moral outcry. Shadwell, for example, harshly criticizes writers who put "debauch'd People upon the Stage," and worse yet, would reward them.[5] Whatever the developments of the later 1670s, the audience could be quite touchy about morality during the first half of the Carolean period.

What did the audience want? This question must have exercised every writer, especially since no very clear trend was visible. At the end of the 1660s four semidistinct types were being championed and tried: (1) the rhymed heroic drama—for example, Dryden's *Conquest of Granada;* (2) heroically inclined comedy—for example, *Secret-Love;* (3) romantic intrigue comedy, usually set abroad, and originally quite serious (for example, Tuke's *Adventures*) but showing a tendency to add ever larger doses of light humor, as in Dryden's *An Evening's Love* (1668); (4) low London comedy—for example, *Sir Salomon.* Anglicized French farce predominated in this category, to the disgust of serious writers like Dryden and Shadwell. Dryden turned to heroic comedy, set abroad; Shadwell aimed at low but satiric comedy, as Wycherley was to do. A writer such as Ravenscroft was to enjoy tremendous success by unabashed indulgence in the farcical and foolish, as in *The Citizen Turn'd Gentleman* (1672), a crude adaptation of *Le Bourgeois Gentilhomme.* But a sense of indecision is apparent right around 1670. The next two years were to see the failure of the heroic-comedy experiment: it simply did not attract much of an audience. The answer, however, was not necessarily more French-style farce. Shadwell's attempt to capitalize on the trend in *The Hypocrite* (evidently a lost version of *Tartuffe*) failed, as did the Earl of Orrery's *Guzman* and *Mr. Anthony* (all in 1669). The old-fashioned romantic tragicomedy was out of favor, as Behn found with her first two plays, *The Forc'd Marriage* (1670) and *The Amorous Prince* (1671). Looking back, we can see plainly that slap-

---

[5] See his prefaces to *The Sullen Lovers* (1668) and *The Royal Shepherdess* (1669).

stick action and the risqué were to be the wave of the future. But at the time this trend was anything but obvious: indeed in comments from several prominent writers one sees a clear revulsion against such devices.

An ambitious outsider might have even less sense of trends than the puzzled professionals, but he (or she) did have some advantages. Because initial runs were short the two theatres needed a lot of new plays, and there were few professional authors producing them. The four principal dramatists of the 1660s were Sir William Davenant (who died in 1668), the Earl of Orrery and Sir Robert Howard (both of whom stopped playwriting after 1669), and Dryden. Edward Howard was an embittered failure about to lapse into silence; the lazy Etherege was not to write his third (and last) play for another six years. The year 1671 saw first efforts from John Crowne, Wycherley, and Elkanah Settle; by 1676, Ravenscroft, Nat. Lee, Thomas Otway, and Durfey had started work. From these writers, plus Dryden, Shadwell, and Behn, were to come the majority of Carolean plays. But in 1670 the market was wide-open: not until 1695, when the resumption of heated theatrical competition once again produced a market for new plays, was the theatre again to be so receptive to the efforts of unknown outsiders. Frances Boothby's *Marcelia,* Aphra Behn's first play, William Joyner's *Roman Empress,* John Corye's *Generous Enemies,* Crowne's *Juliana,* and Edward Revet's *Town-Shifts* are all uneven first efforts which achieved professional production at about this time.

The Frolicks or The Lawyer Cheated

When Elizabeth Polwhele sat down to write in 1670 or 1671, she had several options. We now know that she had already written a rhymed tragedy, *The Faithful Virgins* (ca. 1670), evidently performed by the Duke's Company. One might have expected her to try romantic tragicomedy set abroad, of the sort Aphra Behn started with. Double-plot tragicomedy with an upper-class comic plot line would have been another logical choice. Dryden and James Howard had pioneered the form, and they were imitated by Boothby in

Marcelia. Instead, Polwhele moved all the way to low London comedy—lively, realistic, and distinctly bawdy. "I question not but I shall be taxed for writing a play so comical," she admits in her dedication. For inspiration she had the anglicized French farces—especially Caryll's *Sir Salomon,* Dryden's and the Duke of Newcastle's *Sir Martin Mar-all,* and Betterton's *Amorous Widow.*

The Frolicks is built around two basic plots—an "imaginary cuckold" story, and a "gay couple" elopement with attendant complications. Both are stock situations, handled with flair and originality. The characters are sharply drawn, though they suffer from the superficiality usual in this kind of Restoration comedy. The action is rather loosely handled, especially in the tavern scenes in Act III. In this respect too the play is normal. The coffeehouse scenes in Act III of Sir Thomas St. Serfe's *Tarugo's Wiles* stop the plot action even more fully. Song and dance are major elements in the frothy confection Polwhele whips up: one must remember that this *is* a frolic—a merry romp contrived for boisterous stage performance, not a polished literary gem to be savored in the reader's study. Similarly, a piece such as Ravenscroft's immensely successful *The Citizen Turn'd Gentleman* loses its appeal on the printed page. So would a Chaplin film, reduced to the frigid basics of its scenario.

Technically *The Frolicks* is an intrigue comedy, but Polwhele is little concerned with suspense. The genial tone makes us expect a happy ending, and we get it. The action is hard to summarize, but easy to follow. Basically the events of the play are these: (1) Sir William Meanwell, an ineffectual country gentleman, has married a country girl who is bowled over by the delights of London and handsome young men. Sir William is in constant fear of horning, and his anxiety keeps getting fueled to fever pitch by the dire warnings of his servant, Ralph. No actual cuckolding occurs during the play, though the audience knows very well that Meanwell's suspicions are not without foundation. But he is always won over by his wife's tears and cajolery: time after time we await with relish yet another tidy escape. Finally, at the end of the play,

Meanwell indignantly dismisses Ralph from his service for breeding unworthy suspicions of his wife—a neat and unexpected twist. (2) Lady Meanwell's sister, Faith, is seduced by Lord Courtall, a wealthy rake who leaves his neglected wife in the country. He is assisted in his designs by Procreate, a pseudogenteel French bawd. Courtall is cut out by the dashing Sir Francis Makelove, who hastily marries the lady when Courtall solemnly and untruthfully informs him that she is wealthy. (3) Swallow, a wealthy lawyer, justice of the peace, and moneylender, proposes to marry his witty daughter Clarabell to either Sir Gregory, a nouveau-riche young country knight, or Mr. Zany, a rich heir. Clarabell, however, falls in love with the rakish and bankrupt Rightwit, who manages to trick Swallow into helping them contract a legally unassailable marriage—hence the subtitle of the play. (4) Zany marries Rightwit's sister, Leonora, and Sir Gregory marries Procreate—both thinking that they are marrying Clarabell.

As usual in Restoration comedy, all of these characters are stock figures. Sir Gregory and Zany, like their servants Speak and Plainman, are Jonsonian humour-butts, openly clownish and ridiculous. Old husband, young wife, and lustful gallants were to become a routine formula later in the period: at this date they are by no means the commonplaces they seem, though examples are plentiful in Renaissance drama. The Meanwells' situation is an anticipatory analogue of the Pinchwife story in Wycherley's *Country-Wife* (1675). There the ingenue wife gives a despicable husband the horns he deserves. In both plays the husband is frantic to get his country innocent out of London and away from temptation, but here the husband verges on the pathetic, and the wife is more capable of dissimulation than Margery Pinchwife. Our perspective here is that of the couple, not that of the would-be seducer. The husband is ridiculous, his wife silly—but the conclusion is unusual. An actual cuckolding could turn Meanwell into an unpleasantly pathetic or contemptible object. And at this date such cuckoldings do not occur in Restoration comedies. But though the "happy ending" satisfies us within the play, we are left to realize that the marriage is completely hollow and unsound. Most Restoration comedies gloss over such situations lightly. Here Meanwell's dismissal of Ralph drives home hard, right at the end of the play, the nature of the fool's paradise he is living in. His wife has not actually made him a cuckold, but she will do so when opportunity is to be found.

The handling of the play's three rakes is a study in contrasts. Sir Francis Makelove is an engaging puppy, a cheerful, gullible young man-about-town easily duped by the vindictive Lord Courtall. Makelove gives Lady Meanwell a pretty determined rush, but enjoys cutting Lord Courtall out with Faith. He never discovers his mistake—a handling reminiscent of some of Molière's endings. Few Restoration writers could resist bursting the bubble, as Ravenscroft does so clumsily at the end of *The Citizen Turn'd Gentleman*. We like Makelove well enough that his direct discomfiture would strike a discordant note. The point is deftly handled: the folly of this would-be rake is duly punished, but only in our imagination. Lord Courtall, in contrast, is an effectively drawn scoundrel. He promises Procreate (one of his ex-mistresses) a wealthy country husband if she will help him debauch Faith, and sets Makelove off on his elopement with plausible, effusively "sincere" lies. He gets little stage time, but is made vivid. When we see him grumbling, "I must leave drabbing at these unreasonable French rates" after paying Procreate (II, 248–249), or telling a servant to put away letters from his wife unopened, we react to deft touches which make him an unattractive character. Our dislike serves as an effective contrast to the slavish deference his rank and money command from everyone in the play. However light the tone here and elsewhere, the play does not lack an acute and reflectively satiric view of its characters.

Rightwit, the romantic lead, is a different sort of rake— wild and spendthrift, but sensible and good at heart. The play opens as his sister despairingly reproaches him—he has mortgaged his estate to the hilt and run through £100 in ten days. (In buying power this would be equivalent to at least

$2000 today.) He replies indignantly that he has 8 shillings left. The rest indeed is gone, for "wine and women must be had. . . . Besides there is a law that says . . . that children must not be knock'd i'th' head, and those that get them must keep them" (I, 30–34). Why does he not marry? Simple—he could not think of confining himself to one woman. The exuberant Rightwit belongs to a recognized subtype especially popular in the late 1660s—the "extravagant rake." [6] Obvious prior examples include Welbred in James Howard's *English Mounsieur* and Philidor in his *All Mistaken,* Loveby in Dryden's *Wild Gallant* and Celadon in his *Secret-Love,* Sir Frederick Frollick in Etherege's *Comical Revenge.* This list could be greatly lengthened. We see Rightwit pursued by angry cast mistresses bearing two of his bastards—a trick borrowed from *All Mistaken.* Polwhele develops the gag very cleverly. Rightwit enters with the two bastards tied to his back (squalling lustily). Clarabell, far from being upset, thinks the incident hilarious, and rallies him unmercifully (IV, 143 ff.), though she does untie him. Zany and Sir Gregory promptly rebind him (162 ff.); Clarabell, finding him caught again, teases him into a fury. Escaping with the help of his friend Philario, Rightwit vanishes, muttering imprecations. A little later Clarabell encounters her father, practically foaming at the mouth, with the bastards tied to *his* back. This stunt gets Rightwit incarcerated in the nearest jail, but Clarabell, amused by the trick, promptly springs him in an entertaining escape scene.

When the couple first meet in Act II they are immediately attracted. Rightwit tries his rakish blandishments in a bawdy proposition scene, but getting nowhere starts to find himself seriously interested (II, 62 ff.). In a fine, light-hearted example of the gay-couple love game the pair joke and tease and spar their way through the antics of the tavern scenes, arriving finally at a comic form of the knightly "Test": Clarabell says "I mean not to marry with any man"—but she offers

[6] The subject has been well studied by Robert Jordan, "The Extravagant Rake in Restoration Comedy," *Restoration Literature,* ed. Harold Love (London: Methuen, 1972), pp. 69–90.

a dare. If Rightwit can get her father to cooperate, she will marry him (IV, 445–448). Rightwit swears that he can do it; she replies, "make this good, and I am thine. Otherwise I will never see thy face again" (460–461). Of course he succeeds: well-paid to assist with a clandestine marriage, Swallow is too pleased with himself and his fee to see through the disguises of the participants.

Clarabell belongs to the new breed of heroine—tough, emancipated, and vigorously independent. Her witty banter is more than her grumbling father can keep up with, and the gusto of her practical joking matches even Rightwit's. Slipping out at night in male attire to romp in a local tavern, bewildering her unwelcome suitors, engineering a jailbreak after enlisting the help of Mark, her father's hard-drinking clerk, Clarabell is really the most vivid and dominant figure in the play. Like James Howard's Mirida she participates actively in all the high jinks; she is more than a partner in witty banter. In passing we should point out that the role of Mirida in *All Mistaken* was taken by pretty, witty Nell Gwyn, who would have made a delightful Clarabell and indeed could just have done so. She specialized in gay-couple heroines, including Florimell in *Secret-Love* and the second Constantia in Buckingham's revision of *The Chances* (1667). Her last season with the King's Company was 1670–1671, after which she left the stage.

None of the characters is well enough developed to elicit much feeling from the audience. Clarabell's strongmindedness and verve make her enjoyable, and Rightwit's exuberance makes his rakish past and financial folly emotionally excusable. As was customary early in the Restoration period, there is no real pretense of showing a "reform." A generation later Susanna Centlivre would have had Rightwit down on his knees, piously swearing penitence and constancy, giving the audience an emotional bath in his remorse and good resolutions. But at this date dramatists blithely assume that to marry is to reform. Thus writing in 1671, Dryden defends himself against the charge that he is rewarding "debauched" protagonists in *An Evening's Love:* dramatists, he assures us, "make not vicious persons happy, but only as heaven makes sinners so: that is by reclaiming them first from vice. For so 'tis to be suppos'd they are, when they resolve to marry; for then enjoying what they desire in one, they cease to pursue the love of many." [7] On this basis we are to assume that Rightwit "reforms."

The humour-butts are routinely satirized, but in a cheerful way that carries no real sting. Swallow is technically the "blocking" figure who is pushing Clarabell toward an un- wanted match, but he is never made to seem unpleasant or selfish—compare the father in *Sir Salomon,* or Centlivre's Sir Francis Gripe in *The Busie Body* a generation later. We are always convinced that Clarabell can get her way with Swal- low, and he yields graciously enough at the end. We never sense in him the kind of malignancy which gives a bitter edge to a play such as Wycherley's *Love in a Wood* (1671). The ironies we perceive in the Meanwells' marriage, and in Makelove's snapping up Faith on the matrimonial market, lend an interesting complexity to seemingly formulaic rela- tionships. The injustice done to Ralph is again not typical: we watch with mixed feelings, for though we do not want Lady Meanwell exposed, we know that Ralph is right, and that Meanwell's happy ending has all the substantiality of a house of cards. The one character who is badly handled and underdeveloped is Rightwit's sister, Leonora. Reproaching him at the start of the play, and indignantly rejecting his scheme to get her a wealthy husband, she appears to be a sober version of Clarabell—bright, tough-minded, and in- dependent (II, 318 ff.). She then disappears, and when we find her married to Zany under false pretenses in Act V, we have to be somewhat taken aback. This ending seems dic- tated by symmetry and a desire to dispose neatly of all the characters, not by psychological probability. The original au- dience, to be sure, would have assumed that her cooperation with her brother's scheme was a case of financial necessity overcoming personal preference.

---

[7] Preface to *An Evening's Love* (pub. 1671).

The scene construction of the play has a considerable effect on its impact. To a reader accustomed to the realistic staging of the early twentieth-century theatre, or of Neil Simon today, the series of short, seemingly choppy scenes in *The Frolicks* is very disconcerting and might suggest bad dramaturgy or even lack of visualization of stage production. The play, however, is well considered for the physical conditions of the Restoration stage. The apron, putting actors out amid the audience, made the many "asides" workable: an actor did not have to sidle toward the front edge of a stage and speak out toward the audience, like a villain in a nineteenth-century melodrama. And the sliding wings and shutters parallel to the proscenium arch allowed almost instantaneous scene shifts. (See the illustration.) In the Elizabethan theatre lack of scenery allowed Shakespeare to leap back and forth between Egypt and Rome for scenes of a few lines. One can do this in a movie, but not in the theatre of Ibsen. The changeable scenery of the Restoration stage, however, allowed for almost as much freedom as in pre-Commonwealth drama. Neoclassical concern about the "unities" made authors chary of great leaps through time and space, but within the confines of a house or town, considerable variety was feasible. The result, in *The Frolicks,* is an almost cinematic freedom of motion.[8]

[8] There is still great controversy over the interior design and scenic arrangements in Restoration theatres. The elaborate setup envisaged by John Harrington Smith and Dougald MacMillan requires a series of four dispersed shutters between the proscenium arch and the back of the theatre. (See *The Works of John Dryden,* VIII, ed. Smith and MacMillan [Berkeley: University of California Press, 1962], 307–316.) This interpretation of the famous Wren "section view" of an unidentified playhouse has been sharply criticized in a review by Edward A. Langhans (*Theatre Notebook,* 17 [1963], 94–97), who suggests that the Bridges Street theatre probably had dispersed wings, with shutters only at the back and provision for only a single "inner stage." The degree to which wings and shutters were coordinated remains a matter of dispute. A theatre designed along the lines Langhans suggests is what is shown in our conjectural illustration. For a close scenic analysis of a play staged in a theatre of this type (Lincoln's Inn Fields), see Colin Visser, "The Anatomy of the Early Restoration Stage: *The Adventures of Five Hours* and John Dryden's 'Spanish' Comedies," *Theatre Notebook,* 29 (1975), 56–69, 114–119. For source materials and reconstructions of Restoration theatres, the reader should consult Richard Leacroft, *The Development of the English*

Conjectural reconstruction of an early Restoration theatre.
By Peter Kahn, Cornell University.

This conjectural reconstruction depicts the kind of theatre for which *The Frolicks* was written. The picture is guesswork, an invention based upon contemporary plans and drawings. As a composite picture, it is a plausible approximation of a working English theatre ca. 1670. Very little is known about the interior of the Bridges Street theatre: the evidence has been carefully reviewed by Donald C. Mullin.*

Restoration theatre design was heavily influenced by Italian and French tradition. Serlio and Palladio based their designs on the Vitruvian plan of the Roman theatre: a small interior hall with the audience seated in a semicircular amphitheatre before the stage, a shallow acting space in front of the *scaena frons,* a classical façade, and a raked stage. The "three-dimensional" stage of sixteenth-century Italy developed into the painted wing and shutter stage of seventeenth-century France and Italy. This was the arrangement developed by Inigo Jones for court masques and employed in the public theatre in England after 1660. The classical scene front, according to a sketch by Sir Christopher Wren (plan "81" of Wren's papers at All Souls College, Oxford), becomes a semicircular arc of the proscenium, allowing an area of about twenty feet in width and height for the vista stage with its retractable wings (or, possibly, *periaktoi*), shutters, and an interior stage (not visible here because the center stage shutters are closed), which would "reveal" a deeper stage view.

Another view, a section of a "Play House," also by Wren (and also at All Souls), gives only a glimpse of the permanent proscenium beam, showing more of the "picture frame" proscenium immediately next to a gallery of boxes. In the present illustration the two Wren plans are combined to show the possibility of continuing the audience gallery on the stage proper, where the "boxes" become proscenium doors, musicians' galleries, and acting balconies. The frontispiece to Pierre Perrin's *Ariane* shows the stage of the 1674 Drury Lane theatre. There the stage apron is flattened, and the proscenium is curtained at the top of the proscenium arch. These, then, are the principal sources for the present illustration.

The stage was equipped with at least three sets of grooves for side wings (visible in the cutaway at the left), plus those for the shutters. These allow for quick changes as the wings and shutters are pulled into or out of view. The floor, judging from Wren's sketches, must have been raked on an inclined plane of about ten to fifteen degrees. Top valances are shown in the cutaway: they could be raised or lowered to frame the scene changes all around. No attempt has been made to illustrate the theatre's lighting. Large numbers of tallow candles in brackets and chandeliers supplied illumination, but the evidence about their number and placement is very tenuous.

* "The Theatre Royal, Bridges Street: A Conjectural Restoration," *Educational Theatre Journal,* 19 (1967), 17–29. The reader may also wish to consult Edward A. Langhans, "Pictorial Material on the Bridges Street and Drury Lane Theatres," *Theatre Survey,* 8 (1966), 80–100, and *Survey of London,* XXXV (London: Athlone Press, 1970), chap. 4.

Despite the plenitude of scenes only seven or eight distinct locations are required. They are discussed in order of appearance.

(1) Rightwit's house in London, where the Meanwells stay during their visit. In I, 41.1, a dining table is "discovered," presumably behind the back shutters; in all other cases the place is probably to be deduced by the entrance of appropriate characters (I, 1, II, 260, IV, 19, 94; and V, 83, 188). These scenes could even be played against the proscenium wall with the street shown on the wings and shutters.

(2) A city street. These scenes, beginning at I, 150, IV, 1, 230, 329, 441; and V, 137, 209, were probably played with an unidentified street painted on the wings and the back shutters, though at one point the Strand is mentioned. This arrangement forms the neutral background against which the proscenium walls can be used as different locations.

(3) Swallow's office or reception room in his home (scenes beginning at I, 214; II, 1, 487; IV, 29, 309; and V, 1). Several of these scenes could be played against the proscenium wall to keep the production as simple as possible.

(4) Courtall's lodgings in London (II, 210). Though it is used only once, a view of the rake's dressing room would help differentiate Courtall from the other characters. Or the scene could be played against the proscenium wall.

(5) A tavern (II, 318; III, 1, and 73). Technically, the taverns in Acts II and III are probably different, but no more than a minimal distinction need be made.

(6) Procreate's house (II, 398, 559; IV, 75, 225; and V, 221). In the first, third, and fourth instances this house is "discovered," and benches for courting couples are required. There is an obvious shifting problem at II, 398, when we move here from a tavern scene. The author copes with the difficulty by specifying that the tavern scene end with an antic dance, a cover which could be continued on the fore-

---

Playhouse (London: Methuen, 1973), chaps. 4 and 5, and Donald C. Mullin, *The Development of the Playhouse* (Berkeley: University of California Press, 1970), chap. 5.

stage while the preceding set is cleared. The "new room" in Procreate's house need only be the discovery stage behind the shutters, though from the anticipatory fuss (IV, 82 ff.) we may deduce that the scene of Faith's downfall is very posh indeed.

(7) Another street, away from Rightwit's lodgings and near some "ruins" (scenes beginning at IV, 126). Probably a change would be made only in the back shutters.

(8) A prison (IV, 346). This is a detention cell for gentlemen, not the common room of a Bridewell or Newgate. The Turnkey's room (IV, 414) would probably have been played against the proscenium arch, using the first balcony on the opposite side as the level "above."

As this brief analysis suggests, lively action and movement are contrived within perfectly manageable stage demands. Most if not all of the scenery could be taken from stock: prisons, taverns, and well-appointed houses are all commonplace in the comedy of this period. The stage effects implied in the stage directions are without exception feasible, and the sequence of scenes suggests at least minimal competence in practical theatre matters. There are a few glaring signs of amateurism—for example, at II, 385.1, the musicians enter far too soon after they are sent for, and at III, 155, insufficient time is allowed for a change of clothes. But for the most part the author knew what she was doing. To stage *The Frolicks* today would require some ingenuity and an audience willing to tolerate unfamiliar conventions. On either a "realistic" modern set or the Elizabethan stage the play would not work comfortably. But the reader used to visualizing those theatres must realize that Polwhele was working with a markedly different concept of stagecraft.

Comparing *The Frolicks* with some plays from about the same time, one quickly sees that it is both typical and remarkably forward looking. The London setting, the topographical references, the social level of the characters, the attitudes toward marriage and money are all what one might expect at this date. Putting the heroine in male dress had become a favorite plot element in the sixties, used in play after play. The reader will recall Wycherley's use of the device five years later in *The Country-Wife* and *The Plain-Dealer*. It fosters risqué episodes and allows a titillating display of female legs in tight pants. The further use of transsexual disguise in Act III is rather less usual at this date. First in a dance, and then when Sir Gregory and Zany are arrested and brought up before Swallow as whores, Polwhele adds the sort of touch Sir John Vanbrugh was to capitalize on in *The Provok'd Wife* (1697).

Three plays seem particularly relevant to *The Frolicks*. Wycherley's first effort, *Love in a Wood* (March 1671), has a less developed gay-couple, a multilined plot, and a lower-class element which seems to derive from Jacobean city comedy via a play such as John Wilson's *Cheats* (1663). Wycherley's model obviously was Etherege's first play, *The Comical Revenge, or Love in a Tub* (1664). The sexual element in the piece is old-fashioned, used to degrade the hypocritical participants. Revet's *Town-Shifts, or The Suburb-Justice* (acted by March 1671) has many parallels to Polwhele's play. It possesses a cheerful, lightweight elopement plot, a prison scene, and good-humored intrigue. Socially, the setting is lower, and it has rustic trimmings which have reminded critics of Elizabethan comedy. In type the two plays are quite similar, and the nature of their appeal is much the same. But nothing in Revet's play looks toward the boom in song and dance evident by 1674; the play is quite chaste; and the characters entirely lack the middle and upper-class town air so basic to *The Frolicks*. Polwhele's attitude of tolerant scepticism, especially where the Meanwells, Lord Courtall, and Sir Francis Makelove are concerned, makes her play decisively a thing of the 1670s. She is not writing in the tradition of Middleton and Wilson; she is not following Shadwell along Jonsonian paths. The lightness of tone, like the avoidance of large doses of raw sex, is rather pleasant. John Dover's *The Mall* (1674), Wycherley's *Country-Wife*, Thomas (?) Rawlins' *Tom Essence* (1676), and a host of other sex comedies have their own appeal, but lack the decency of *The Frolicks*. Polwhele's play is far from chastely innocent, but by no means are we in the world of *Mr. Limberham*. A play quite similar in setting and outlook is Nevil Payne's *Morning Ramble* (acted by November 1672), an even lighter-weight romp through London. A duel, gaming-house episodes, dashing young women abroad in men's clothes in the middle of the night—all are heaped together in a pleasant confection. There is too little action to make a really good play; talk outweighs plot. In part, Payne's trifle is held together by the obvious relevance of the duel to topical events—Thomas Otway's angry challenge to Elkanah Settle over a scurrilous poem.[9]

Personal satire had become quite common in "London" comedies, and Polwhele hastens to disavow any such intent: "I must declare it is free from abusing any person" (dedication). Any comedy so full of topographical references might well set the audience to wondering just who a rascally old lawyer or a womanizing spendthrift might be. A few years later Dryden complained:

> Fools you will have, and rais'd at vast expence,
> And yet as soon as seen, they give offence.
> Time was, when none would cry, that Oaf was mee.[10]

A number of plays around 1670 containing nasty personal satire had caused some major scandals. In *The Sullen Lovers* (May 1668) Shadwell put Sir Robert Howard on stage as Sir Positive At-all, an insufferably arrogant know-it-all who gets married off to someone else's pregnant whore. Edward Howard appears in the same play as the poet Ninny. In January 1669 the actor Edward Kynaston was "severely beaten with sticks" by hired thugs for "taking off" the foppish Sir Charles Sedley in a performance of Newcastle's *Heiress*. In February and March 1669 the whole government of England was rocked by the scandal which followed when Sir Robert Howard and the Duke of Buckingham attempted to burlesque a fellow Privy Council member in *The Country Gentleman*—a

---

[9] For an account of this neglected play, see Montague Summers, *The Playhouse of Pepys* (1935; rpt. New York: Humanities Press, 1964), pp. 392–394.

[10] Prologue to Shadwell's *A True Widow* (1678).

play which Charles II himself suppressed.[11] Shadwell's second play, *The Humorists,* was finally staged in December 1670 after the censor forced major revamping. In his preface to the published version Shadwell proclaimed his injured innocence and denied "personation," but the manuscript of the original does not seem to bear him out.[12] In December 1671 Buckingham's famous savaging of Dryden in *The Rehearsal* finally reached the stage—a play which appears also to contain some sharp political digs at the Earl of Arlington. Personal satire had become a game. John Aubrey wrote to Anthony à Wood, 26 October 1671, that he was writing a comedy for Shadwell to get staged—"but of this, mum! for tis very satyricall against some of my mischievous enemies." Alas, the piece was not completed.[13] *The Frolicks* is evidently free of personal attacks. But Polwhele probably meant to keep her identity concealed, and an anonymous play full of local topography and pointed cracks at some of its characters would have been viewed with speculative suspicion.

We would make no extravagant claims for the literary merits of *The Frolicks.* It is the work of an intelligent young playwright learning her trade. The author uses stock elements in mostly well proven ways, though in small details and touches of character there are signs of real flair and skill. The avoidance of black and white in character and the restraint shown at the end bespeak a subtlety Ravenscroft could have used to advantage. As a work of literature the play is clearly scrappy, superficial, and lacking significant form—as are most plays of the time. The Restoration theatre was everyday amusement for certain segments of London society—a kind of cross between movies or television and a ball park. Orange women hawked their wares, whores plied

[11] On this play and its repercussions, see Arthur H. Scouten and Robert D. Hume, *The Country Gentleman: A "Lost" Play and Its Background* (Philadelphia: University of Pennsylvania Press, 1976).

[12] The manuscript, preserved in the Portland Papers now on loan to the Nottingham University Library, is being edited by Richard Perkin.

[13] *Brief Lives,* ed. Andrew Clark, 2 vols. (Oxford: Clarendon Press, 1898), I, 52n.

their trade, society types came to see and be seen. The admission system was such that one could get in for a while (an act or so) without paying. In consequence people drifted in and out. By contrast, a Boston Pops audience would seem sedate and attentive. Critics in search of theme and "meaning" tend to forget how easily Pepys is charmed by an isolated scene, character, jig, song—or shapely female leg. *The Frolicks* must be judged as a lively stage vehicle well contrived to amuse its audience. The lavish use of song and dance, the rapid succession of skitlike scenes, the horseplay, all remain dead on the printed page. In the theatre, boisterously performed, they could serve as the basis for an entertaining romp. The play is indeed just what its author calls it—a series of frolics.

The Manuscript and Its Provenance

The manuscript comprises 96 leaves (17.5 x 14 cm.). Three kinds of paper were used. The outer, blank leaves and the title page are a Spanish paper with a coat of arms watermark.[14] The rest of the manuscript uses two lighter-weight papers, apparently at random—one the familiar horn and baldric, the other a Spanish paper with an eagle watermark.[15] The binding is very similar to that produced by the Court binder for Charles II; it was carefully repaired in 1974.

The play occupies leaves 5r through 89v. The title page occupies 1r, the dedication 2r through 3v; an incomplete list of "Persons" appears on 90v—evidently an afterthought. An autograph signature ("Arthur Hewes") dated 1681 appears on 4r. Cropping has affected twenty-six words, mostly late in the

[14] See Edward Heawood, *Watermarks Mainly of the 17th and 18th Centuries*, Monumenta Chartæ Papyraceæ, I (Hilversum, Holland: Paper Publications Society, 1950), #739, 741, 763, and pl. 118. His examples from English documents are dated 1669–1673.
[15] For the former compare Heawood #2673, p. 123, and pl. 340. For the eagle paper see W. A. Churchill, *Watermarks in Paper in Holland, England, France, Etc., in the XVII and XVIII Centuries* (Amsterdam: Menno Hertzberger, 1935), #443, p. 85, and plate. His examples of use in English manuscripts range from 1632 to 1673.

play, but nothing of significance has been lost thereby. The last six leaves are blank, though staining of the sort which defaced 5r appears on 91v and 92r.

The manuscript basically is in fine condition. Unfortunately the first page of Act I is badly damaged; we could only speculate about the cause of such disfiguring and localized staining. With the manuscript we found an attempt at a transcription of the page, written on a piece of cheap blue paper and signed "A.G." (identity unknown). From paper and hand we would guess that this document is to be dated ca. 1900. Close study of the damaged page shows that A.G. made several errors and in at least one case seriously distorted the sense of the text. He admits, indeed, that "The four last lines are very doubtful, but it requires some high flown figures to correspond with what precedes and follows.—*Little fool,* too, may not be the words of the text, but are submitted as appropriate." Though he may have been able to read words now unrecoverable we have preferred to reject his conjectures entirely and to work from the original alone. No more than six to eight words are entirely obliterated; we have supplied the minimum connectives demanded by the sense. For a fuller account of the problems involved, the reader may consult the Textual Notes.

Almost everything we know about authorship, possible performance, and the circumstances of composition must be deduced from the front matter in the manuscript. The title page reads: "The Frolick's: | or The Lawyer Cheated, | An new Comedey, the | "'first Coppy'" | written by M^{rs}: E:P. | | 1671." The dedication to Prince Rupert is signed "E. Polewheele," and the writer refers to herself as "an unfortunate young woman . . . haunted with poetic devils." The phraseology of the dedication suggests that the author hoped for assistance in getting the play staged. Why else would she "commit" it to the dedicatee, who can "spurn it into nothing" if it does not please him?

Prince Rupert was by no means a bad choice if the author wanted an influential patron. Rupert was an old friend and fellow cavalier exile of Thomas Killigrew, principal owner and

manager of the King's Company. Indeed Killigrew had dedicated his last play to Rupert.[16] And Rupert's mistress was
the beautiful Margaret Hughes (or Hewes), who acted major
roles for the King's Company from 1668 to Spring 1670,
when Rupert removed her from the stage. What influence
she may have had with her old troupe one can only guess,
but Rupert was one of the leading political and military figures in England during the reign of Charles II, and a word
from him to his friend Killigrew would probably have had
some weight.

Margaret Hughes may well have had some share in the
play's fate. The manuscript contains the autograph signature
"Arthur Hewes 1681" (leaf 4r) and his bookplate. Who is this
person? A sale catalogue description of this manuscript
pasted in the front cover (probably by Loewy) says that he
was "probably a son of Mrs. Margaret Hewes (or Hughes) the
actress." However Margaret Hughes is not known to have
had a son. Her only known child, Ruperta, was the daughter
she bore Prince Rupert in 1673. In a will dated December
1682 Rupert divided his estate between "Margaret Hewes
and . . . Ruperta, my naturall daughter begotten on the
bodie of the said Margaret Hewes." [17] Probably then Arthur
Hewes was not a son of Margaret. Edward Langhans has
pointed out to us, however, that Margaret did have a
brother—Christian name unknown, but evidently not the
actor William Hughes. All we know of this brother is that he
was a servant of Prince Rupert, and that according to a gos-
sipy letter dated 20 June 1670 he was "killed" in a brawl,
"upon a dispute" whether Nell Gwyn or Margaret Hughes
"was the handsomer." But such reports are frequently unre-
liable, and to find the manuscript, dedicated to Rupert, in the

---

[16] See Alfred Harbage, *Thomas Killigrew* (1930; rpt. New York: Blom,
1967), p. 104.

[17] This information is based on the entry which will appear in Philip H.
Highfill, Jr., Kalman A. Burnim, and Edward A. Langhans, *A Biographical
Dictionary of Actors, Actresses, Musicians, Dancers, Managers and Other
Stage Personnel in London, 1660–1800*, 14 vols. in progress (Carbondale:
Southern Illinois University Press, 1973—   ). Edward Langhans very kindly
made an advance copy available to us.

hands of a "Hewes" does suggest the theatrical connection.

Was the play acted? No performance record is known, but that means very little. Records of the two companies are frustratingly incomplete in the Restoration period, especially in the years 1669–1672 after Pepys ended his *Diary*. For more than one hundred new plays in the Restoration our only evidence of performance comes from publication—the inclusion of prologue, epilogue, and a cast list is good evidence of actual production.[18] So lack of other evidence means little either way. That the play was meant to be performed there can be no doubt; whether the author achieved her aim we shall probably never know. One piece of evidence does seem greatly to increase the likelihood: as we will explain in the next section, Polwhele had already had a tragedy staged by the Duke's Company.

What happened to the manuscript between 1681 and the middle of the nineteenth century remains a mystery. What we know of the provenance is this. At some time in the 1840s or 1850s it came into the hands of J. O. Halliwell-Phillipps, an insatiable collector. As the *Dictionary of National Biography* observes, "in youth he found rare volumes 'plenty as blackberries' on the outside stalls of old bookshops," and he bought rare books and manuscripts by the thousands, selling them off at auction to pay for fresh purchases. *The Frolicks* has been known to theatre historians principally from an entry in the work popularly known as "Halliwell's *Dictionary*":

> THE FROLIC. The Frolick; or, the Lawyer Cheated, a new comedy by E.P., "an unfortunate younge woman haunted by poetick divills," 1671, dedicated to Prince Rupert. In manuscript, and unpublished.[19]

That Halliwell-Phillipps had owned the manuscript is easily proved. A Sotheby and Wilkinson sale catalogue (23 May

[18] See Judith Milhous and Robert D. Hume, "Dating Play Premières from Publication Data, 1660–1700," *Harvard Library Bulletin,* 22 (1974), 374–405.

[19] James O. Halliwell [-Phillipps], *A Dictionary of Old English Plays* (London: John Russell Smith, 1860), p. 105.

1856) of miscellaneous Halliwell-Phillipps books ("a very valuable and important collection of Shaksperian & dramatic literature") contains as item #299, "Polwheele (Elizabeth) The Frolick, or the Lawyer Cheated. . . . An amusing comedy of intrigue, with allusions to London localities, songs, catches, &c." According to an annotated copy of the catalogue, the purchaser was Joseph "Lilly" (a bookseller, d. 1870), the price "2/19/0." [20] The earliest scholarly reference we know to the play is a query by R. Inglis, who had evidently seen the sale catalogue: *"Polwhele's 'Frolick'—*In a catalogue of Shaksperian and dramatic literature, I observed a MS. piece, with the following title: *The Frolick, or, the Lawyer cheated,* a new comedy by E. P. Elizabeth Polwhele. . . . Is anything known regarding the authoress?" [21] There was no public reply.

Directly or indirectly the manuscript came into the possession of the Reverend Francis John Stainforth. In July 1867 it was sold by Sotheby, Wilkinson, and Hodge as part of Stainforth's collection of "Works of British and American Poetesses, and Female Dramatic Writers." An annotated copy of the sale catalogue in the New York Public Library tells us that the buyer was the eccentric bookseller George Bumstead; the price, 7 shillings. At some point the manuscript then passed into the hands of F. A. Marshall, whose bookplate it now bears. Frank Marshall was a well-known man of the theatre, and coeditor (with Henry Irving) of a popular edition of Shakespeare. After his death the manuscript was once again sold by Sotheby, Wilkinson, and Hodge (June 1890). According to an annotated copy of the sale catalogue the buyer was "Jarvis" (a bookseller); the price, 13 shillings.[22] The manuscript must have been sold at least once more, this time out of a priced catalogue, since someone—presumably Benno Loewy—pasted into the manuscript a cutting with the following description, more elaborate than any which appears in the 1856, 1867, or 1890 catalogues:

[20] Microfilm in the Folger Library (British Library copy).
[21] *Notes and Queries,* 2d ser., 7 (1859), 279–280.
[22] Annotated copy in the British Library.

"The Frolicks; or The Lawyer Cheated," a New Comedy, the first copy written by Mrs. E.P., 1671, 4to, *morocco*. [Price cut away.]

The authoress, Mistress E. Polwhele, dedicates the work, in very high flown language, to Prince Rupert. She apologizes for her presumption in doing so, and tells him that she is "an unfortunate young woman . . . haunted with poetick divells." Halliwell notices this work in *Dict. Old Plays*, as existing only in MS.

It may be presumed that this, the original MS., was bound by the Court binder (for it is in the red morocco, similar to Charles II.'s books), and then sent to Prince Rupert, from whom it would appear never to have been returned for printing, as it has the bookplate on cover of one Arthur Hewes, Esq., probably a son of Mrs. Margaret Hewes (or Hughes) the actress, who was mistress to Prince Rupert. It has also the autograph signature *Arthur Hewes*, 1681, on a flyleaf.

The price was deliberately cut out of the clipping. Thus far we have had no luck in discovering where Loewy obtained the manuscript.

At some point in this progression the manuscript vanished from scholarly view. It may have been known to W. Carew Hazlitt; in his revision of Halliwell's *Dictionary* he expanded the author's name to "Elizabeth Polwhele" and added the slightly misleading information that the play "is divided into acts and scenes." [23] Early in the present century, however, scholars lost track of the manuscript's whereabouts. Allardyce Nicoll says tersely that Halliwell "records a manuscript of this play," and leaves the matter at that.[24] The most authoritative guide to manuscript matters, the Harbage-Schoenbaum *Annals*, states that the play is by Elizabeth Polwhele, that it is an unacted comedy, and that it is "lost." [25]

---

[23] W. Carew Hazlitt, *A Manual for the Collector and Amateur of Old English Plays* (1892; rpt. New York: Burt Franklin, 1966), p. 92. Hazlitt may have adopted the Christian name from an entry in *Bibliotheca Cornubiensis*, by George Clement Boase and William Prideaux Courtney, 3 vols. (London: Longmans, 1874–1882), where "Elizabeth Polwhele" is credited with "The Frolick or the lawyer defeated" (II; 506). Or he may have been following the 1856 Halliwell-Phillipps sale catalogue.

[24] Allardyce Nicoll, *A History of English Drama 1660–1900*, rev. ed., 6 vols. (Cambridge: Cambridge University Press, 1952–1959), I, 424.

[25] *Annals of English Drama 975–1700*, comp. Alfred Harbage, rev. S. Schoenbaum (London: Methuen, 1964), pp. 168–169.

We know now, of course, that Loewy bequeathed it to Cornell in 1919—and there it has remained ever since, correctly catalogued. No one at Cornell had reason to suppose that it was "lost" or of any interest. No theatre historian had reason to inquire after it there.

Polwhele's *Faithful Virgins*

The Frolicks was not a unique effort from a stagestruck amateur, as one might very reasonably presume from reading Halliwell and Hazlitt. In the dedication of *The Frolicks* Polwhele admits her temerity in writing a play of this kind: "I question not but I shall be taxed for writing a play so comical, but those that have ever seen my *Faithful Virgins* and my *Elysium* will justify me a little for writing this." What her "Elysium" is we do not know: a religious masque would be a plausible guess. But in the Bodleian there is in manuscript an anonymous tragedy called "The faithfull Virgins" (MS. Rawl. Poet. 195, ff. 49–78).[26]

The case for attribution rests on three points: (1) the claim to "my faythfull Virgins" in the dedication of *The Frolicks;* (2) the handwriting, which is both identical and highly characteristic. *The Faithful Virgins* is a fair copy, while *The Frolicks* manuscript is the author's "first copy," done less carefully on smaller paper; (3) the initials "E.P." on folio 78v of *The Faithful Virgins*. This page seems to have served as a scratch sheet. Several trial sentences are started (for example, "My Lord pray remember me when you"), but the last entry reads: "Lord Jesus rescue my soule Amen, EP." The form and unusual flourish of the initials is twice very nearly duplicated in the front matter of *The Frolicks*. Consequently we may say with fair assurance that *The Faithful Virgins* is also Polwhele's work, and that it precedes *The Frolicks* chronologically.

The Faithful Virgins was almost certainly given a professional production. On folio 49r appears the following notation: "This Tragedy apoynted to be acted by the dukes Com-

---

[26] The spelling in the running title varies about equally, faithfull/faythfull.

pany of Actors only leaving out what was Cross'd by Henry Herbertt M:R." The theatre companies did not pay Herbert's stiff £2 licensing fee for new plays unless they were serious about performing them. From the limited evidence available in other cases we may infer that licenses were applied for very late—during rehearsals. Scholars have generally taken a license as presumptive evidence of performance—correctly, we believe. Two points about this license are problematical: it is not in Herbert's handwriting, and it is not dated, as was Herbert's practice. Montague Summers, in the only analysis of the manuscript known to us, concluded that "it is a fair copy, licence and all, from the original script, which was used as the prompt copy." [27] The manuscript is indubitably a fair copy, license included, but nothing beyond conjecture suggests that the original script was used as a prompt copy. And Summers errs in asserting that only four lines were cut by the censor. As we read the passages affected, five lines were cut on 52v, two lines on 76r. [28]

The date of *The Faithful Virgins* has been the subject of considerable confusion, and might seem to cast doubt on our attribution. The *Annals* says that it was performed by the Duke's Company "1661–1663." The editors of *The London Stage* enter the play under June 1663 with the comment that the manuscript "bears a permit to be acted by the Duke's Company . . . signed [sic] by Henry Herbert. Since Herbert retired in July 1663, the play . . . can be dated from about 1661 to June 1663." [29] Summers makes exactly the same deduction. This dating is, however, fallacious. Herbert did not "retire" in July 1663; rather, he appears to have leased his office as Master of the Revels to his assistant, Edward Hayward, for an indeterminate period. [30] Herbert did not die

[27] *The Playhouse of Pepys*, pp. 338–341.

[28] On the cover page (49r), under the license, appears the following comment: "the Chaster witts, say; that ⌊luxury⌋must be pronounc'ed for letchery in the masque throughout. acording wthe judgement off—Docter, H:C:." The identity of Doctor H.C. remains a puzzle.

[29] *The London Stage*, pt. 1, p. 65.

[30] See *The Dramatic Records of Sir Henry Herbert,* ed. Joseph Quincy Adams (New Haven: Yale University Press, 1917), esp. pp. 126–129.

until 1673, and he must have resumed full exercise of his office prior to April 1667, when he licensed Edward Howard's *Change of Crownes*.[31] Consequently Herbert's license is useless in dating *The Faithful Virgins*. Herbert was definitely still licensing plays as late as the time of *The Frolicks*. Edward Langhans has pointed out to us that prompt copies of William Cartwright's *Ordinary* and *Lady Errant* were licensed for production in 1672: the licenses are dated 15 January and 9 March 1671 (that is, 1671/2), and both are signed by Herbert.[32] Hence all we can say with assurance about the date of *The Faithful Virgins* is that it was probably written at least several months earlier than March 1671/2, the last time at which *The Frolicks* could have been dated 1671. Performance ca. 1670 seems likely: even then the author was probably quite young.

Comparing Polwhele's two plays, one has to be impressed with the author's audacity in striking out so vigorously in different directions. *The Faithful Virgins* is in most respects an extremely old-fashioned play. Its clanking rhyme is a concession to 1660s style; otherwise, like William Killigrew's sodden plays, it is largely a throwback to types popular in the 1620s and 1630s. The handling is not without imagination, but one cannot call the results as a whole better than poor. The high-flown *précieuse* sentiment which pervades the play lacks conviction: the author seems much more comfortable with the everyday setting and sentiments of *The Frolicks*.

The story, in brief, is this. The play opens, rather mysteriously, with Merantha and Umira keeping vigil over a hearse—faithful virgins lamenting the demise of Philammon. Umira's brother Statenor visits the hearse and falls madly in

---

[31] Notation on the MS prompt copy: "This Tragicomedy called the Change of Crownes May be Acted: Aprill 13th 1667. Henry Herbert M R." See *The Change of Crownes*, ed. Frederick S. Boas (London: Oxford University Press, 1949), p. 89. The play received its premiere 15 April.

[32] These prompt copies were once owned by T. W. Baldwin, and are commented upon in *The Plays and Poems of William Cartwright*, ed. G. Blakemore Evans (Madison: University of Wisconsin Press, 1951), pp. 85, 260. Evans assumes that 1671 (not 1671/2) is meant. However 15 January was a Sunday in 1671, so 1672 seems likelier.

love with Merantha (the "killing eyes" convention is employed here). He proposes to woo her by proxy via his page,
"Floradine," who is very distressed about it. The reason is not
far to seek: Floradine is in fact Philammon's sister Erasila,
serving Statenor in male attire and deeply in love with him.
Along the way we learn that the nobly-born Cleophon has
been engaged to Isabella, who throws him over in order to
marry the lecherous Duke of Tuscany—the marriage occur-
ring at the end of Act I, with an Elizabethan-style dumb
show. In Act II the disappointed Cleophon consults a pair of
witches in a cave. In the midst of apparitions, thunder, song,
and dance—highly reminiscent of Davenant's tarted-up version of *Macbeth*—the witches prophesy that he will become
Duke of Tuscany, though he will never win Isabella. Act III
is largely taken up with an elaborate masque. The allegorical
figures include Detraction, Envy, Ambition, Letchery, Chas-
tity, Pride, Flattery, Avarice, Drunkenness (and five dancing
drunks), Virtue, Humility, Patience, Justice, Prudence, Sobri-
ety, and a stray angel. Virtue pointedly ascribes social reform
to the example of the Duke and Duchess. One can scarcely
help wondering what Polwhele thought of Charles II; this
could be read as rather pointed ironic commentary.

In Act IV we discover that the Duke is smitten with Umira.
She virtuously rejects his advances, whereupon he plans to
abduct her. The Duchess gets wind of the matter and
promptly persuades her admirer Trasilius to murder Umira.
In the final act he does so, and a general melee follows.
Cleophon kills Trasilius. Statenor kills the Duke but is fatally
wounded himself. Merantha kills herself, disgusted with this
wicked world. Floradine-Erasila stabs herself when she sees
Statenor dying, and expires. Cleophon is acknowledged as
the new Duke of Tuscany and takes charge. The curtain is
dropped and "Solemn musique" is played while bodies are
carried off. Then "The Scean Open's" and we discover the
bodies of Umira, Merantha, and Erasila dead on a couch—
faithful virgins all. Statenor's head rests in Erasila's lap. On
the other side of the bier are laid Trasilius and the Duke.
Having brought in the Duchess, Cleophon berates her for the

results of her wicked vengeance. But he still loves her, and recognizes the provocation, so he merely ships her off to a "monastery," and proclaims that the faithful virgins will be ever more extolled.

One cannot say a great deal in defense of this lumbering bloodbath. In Cyril Tourneur's hands the characters might have come to life. Not surprisingly the novice writer entirely fails to achieve the somber power with which Tourneur or John Webster would have infused such material. Polwhele had evidently been reading Jacobean and Caroline drama: the "platonic" sentiment is reminiscent of Davenant's early plays, and indeed Summers discerns a specific borrowing from *Albovine* in Act V. The Duke-Duchess part of the play has some parallels to Lope de Vega's *El castigo sin venganza* (*Justice without Revenge*), which might have been known to the authoress, directly or through some intermediary source, though that story verges on the commonplace. The Duke's "unbridled red-hot eroticism" (in Summers' phrase) is made vivid. Judging from Pepys' reaction to Sir Robert Howard's *Duke of Lerma* (1668) an informed theatre-goer could well have viewed Polwhele's Duke as an unsubtle hit at Charles II.

One might ask why, if Polwhele were so up-to-date with *The Frolicks*, she should follow old-fashioned models here? The answer is that tragedy as such was out of fashion in the 1660s. Thomas Porter's *Villain* (1662) is an almost unique exercise in Jacobean blood and thunder. The closest analogues to the type Polwhele tried are Henry Cary's (?) *The Mariage Night*, a Websteresque court-sex melodrama which ends bloodily, and two sprawling tragicomedies by Robert Stapylton, *The Slighted Maid* and *The Step-Mother*. All three were staged in 1663, though the "Cary" play probably dates from the 1630s. Serious drama in the 1660s was mostly devoted to rhymed heroic plays, many of which are happy-ending displays of heroic valor. Polwhele was probably wise in not undertaking to concoct an Almanzor. *The Faithful Virgins* is no success, but Summers was fair in concluding that it presents features of historical interest, and in observing that "being baldly told in outline it probably may appear weaker than it actually is." Even amid the conventional balderdash the play relies on, Polwhele's gusto is apparent.

Some Questions of Authorship

About "E. Polewheele" we know practically nothing. According to the dedication of *The Frolicks,* its author was young, female, and stagestruck. We have discovered no record of any individual with this name who has a demonstrable connection to playwriting or the theatre. Our biographical researches apparently agree with those of nineteenth-century investigators—the 1856 sale catalogue, the *Bibliotheca Cornubiensis,* and Hazlitt all dub the lady Elizabeth. To what extent they derive from one another there is now no way to determine.

The only candidate we can offer is a rather startling one. An Elizabeth Polwhele was the daughter of Theophilus Polwhele, vicar of Tiverton (?–1689), a prominent nonconformist minister. He entered Emmanuel College, Cambridge, in March or April 1644, receiving his B.A. in 1647/8, his M.A. in 1651. He contracted the first of his three marriages in May 1650. Obviously his eldest daughter, Elizabeth, could have been born ca. 1651 and would have been about twenty years old in 1671.[33] Elizabeth Polwhele married the Reverend Stephen Lobb (another nonconformist divine of Cornish extraction) at an unknown date, but well before 17 August 1678, when she bore him a son, one of their five known children. Stephen Lobb was a major ecclesiastical figure in the 1680s, whose willingness to voice his principles made him important friends in the government, but also got him mixed up in the Rye House plot (June 1683). He was later one of the nonconformists who encouraged James II's policy of religious toleration. Elizabeth Polwhele Lobb died in 1691, and Samuel

[33] Mary Polwhele (Theophilus' second wife), in a will dated 7 April 1671, bequeathed "to my son in law [Isaac] Polwheele and my daughter in law [i.e., stepdaughter] Elizabeth Polwheele one hundred Pounds to be paid them when they shall accomplish the age of one and twenty years or be married respectively." Prerogative Court of Canterbury, Wills & Administrations, 1671, f. 147 (microfilm copy in Public Record Office).

Slater preached a funeral sermon on her. Unhappily nothing is to be learned from it, since as Slater notes in his preface, he had been sick and was forced to use a sermon originally preached for someone else. Presumably Slater would not have mentioned so disreputable an occupation as playwriting even had he known of it.[34] In 1757, Theophilus Lobb (one of Elizabeth's sons) was to publish "An Answer To that Important Question, Whether it is lawful for the Professors of the Christian Religion to go to Plays?" His answer was a thunderous No.

Further biographical researches have proved futile to date. Theophilus Polwhele and Stephen Lobb were considerable figures in their day. Histories of dissenting clergy and records of the "ejected" ministers produce numerous references to them. Tracing them we learned quite a lot about the checkered history of the dissenting clergy under Charles II, but, alas, nothing whatever about Elizabeth Polwhele Lobb or her possible playwriting. We can only hope that some future scholar will be lucky enough to come upon letters or diaries which might definitively establish the author's identity. One must grant that a virgin daughter from a very religious nonconformist family makes an odd candidate for the authorship of so racy and au courant a play as *The Frolicks*. Yet to date no alternative has been found,[35] and such a background might explain some things. Failure to publish either play

[34] This biographical information is drawn from the following sources: [George E. Eland], *The Lobb Family from the Sixteenth Century* (Oxford: Oxford University Press, 1955), esp. pp. 11, 20–30; Martin Dunsford, *Historical Memoirs of the Town and Parish of Tiverton* (Exeter: printed for the author by T. Brice, 1790), esp. p. 331; Walter Wilson, *The History and Antiquities of Dissenting Churches,* 4 vols. (London: W. Button, 1810), III, 436–446; *Alumni Cantabrigienses,* comp. John Venn and J. A. Venn (Cambridge: Cambridge University Press, 1924), pt. 1, III, 376–377; A. G. Matthews, *Calamy Revised* (Oxford: Clarendon Press, 1934), pp. 393–394; Samuel Slater, *A Funeral Sermon preached on Mrs. Lobb* (London, 1691), British Library 1417.d.47.

[35] We have, of course, looked for female Polwheles with theatrical connections. As such, there are none. Edward Langhans has pointed out to us that the musician Paul Wheeler is apparently sometimes referred to as Polwhele. We have no information about his family, however. Nonetheless he seems to represent a possible lead toward an alternative candidate.

might be accounted for by the lady's reluctance to expose her ungodly doings more fully, and her later silence would be a logical result of marriage to a respectable young clergyman. We must remember also that antitheatre prejudices hardened only somewhat later in the seventeenth century. Reacting to the outcry of the Collier era we tend to forget that even non-Anglican clergymen did occasionally attend the theatre in the 1660s.

In 1670 female writers were regarded much the way Samuel Johnson viewed female preachers a century later: one marveled that the dog could walk on its hind legs at all. Some people found the performance remarkable; others considered it an unnatural act. There was almost no precedent for an aspiring young woman to look to. Margaret Cavendish, Duchess of Newcastle (1623–1673), had indeed published a stack of unactable closet dramas, among her multitudinous writings, and there were rumors that *The Humorous Lovers,* acted by the Duke's Company in March 1667, was her play, though it was actually her husband's. Her wealth, position, and beauty allowed her exceptional liberty, though they did not prevent her acquiring the nickname "Mad Madge." [36] Reading Pepys' *Diary* for the period of her visit to London in the spring of 1667, one finds in him a curious blend of fascination, astonishment, and scoffing dismissal. Her request to be invited to a meeting of the Royal Society (carried narrowly after heated debate) set the town on its head. Her playwriting and love of science aside, her outlandish dress and behavior left no doubt that she was eccentric, however indubitably brilliant.[37] And she could not readily serve as a viable role-model for a stagestruck commoner.

[36] See Henry Ten Eyck Perry, *The First Duchess of Newcastle and Her Husband as Figures in Literary History* (Boston: Ginn, 1918), and A. S. Turberville, *A History of Welbeck Abbey and Its Owners,* I (London: Faber, 1938).

[37] Although no one seems to have noticed the possibility before, we suspect that *The Poetess* (anonymous, lost), staged by the King's Company in October 1667, may have been a burlesque of Mad Madge, inspired by her much publicized visit the preceding spring. See Judith Milhous and Robert D. Hume, "Lost English Plays, 1660–1700," *Harvard Library Bulletin,* 25 (1977), 5–33.

The most successful woman writer prior to the redoubtable
Aphra Behn was clearly Katherine Philips (1632–1664). A
shy, retiring amateur, she won high praise, even idolatry, for
some very ordinary verse.[38] Perhaps, as Jean Gagen suggests,
she was so lionized because she was both a poetess (hence a
freak) and a self-effacing amateur.[39] She insisted vehemently
that she never wrote a line for publication; the "cruel Ac-
cident" of unauthorized publication in 1662 sent her to her
bed in a state of physical collapse; in 1664 she made her
friends take legal action against a publisher who was proposing to print without permission from copies of her poems
circulating in manuscript. The reasons for the nonpublica-
tion of Polwhele's plays are possibly no farther to seek than
the absolute horror of public exposure felt by Katherine Philips. "Orinda's" only ventures into the theatre were transla-
tions. In 1663 her version of Corneille's *Pompée* was staged
in Dublin, a production arranged by high-born friends over
her ineffectual protests. She seems to have been half-glad,
half-embarrassed. Staged in London later that spring, the
play promptly drew a travesty in Act V of Davenant's medley,
The Play-house to be Let (August 1663). Langbaine remarks
that in later years he saw the Philips *Pompey* acted with
Davenant's skit added as an afterpiece.[40] Her translation of
Corneille's *Horace*, completed after her death by Sir John
Denham, was mounted by the King's Company in 1669. Perhaps the actors did not think much of it. Pepys' comment is
instructive: "a silly Tragedy; but Lacy hath made a farce
of several dances, between each act, one. But his words
are but silly, and invention not extraordinary . . . only
some Dutchmen come out of the mouth and tail of a Ham-
burgh sow" (19 January 1669). Philips had found some
noisy detractors among the "court wits," and one wonders

---

[38] See Philip Webster Souers, *The Matchless Orinda* (Cambridge, Mass.:
Harvard University Press, 1931).

[39] On Philips and the position of "The Lady Writer" see Jean Elisabeth
Gagen, *The New Woman* (New York: Twayne, 1954), chap. 5.

[40] Gerard Langbaine, *An Account of the English Dramatick Poets* (1691),
intro. John Loftis, 2 vols. (Los Angeles: Augustan Reprint Society, 1971), II,
405.

whether the actors might have shared their derisory opinion.

Perhaps Katherine Philips was an inspiration to young Elizabeth Polwhele, though we see no sign of it. More possibly, the production of Frances Boothby's *Marcelia* in the spring of 1669 set her to work, if she had not already written *The Faithful Virgins*. *Marcelia* is an old-fashioned, split-plot tragicomedy of no particular merit. It was published in 1670 with the author's name on the title page: we know nothing else of her. Aphra Behn's first play, *The Forc'd Marriage*, was acted by the Duke's Company in September 1670. She alone among early women writers wrote for bread, as she was bluntly to admit in the preface to *Sir Patient Fancy* (1678). Reading her prefaces, dedications, prologues, and epilogues, one realizes that she was the target of a steady stream of mockery and derogation. She replied with spirit and persevered from necessity, but she had to survive a lot of hard knocks in eking out a bare subsistence as a professional writer. Unlike the genteel and retiring Philips, Behn competed with men as an equal.

Rather surprisingly, no new women dramatists appeared until 1695, when a young lady signing herself "Ariadne" wrote *She Ventures and He Wins*, a flat failure. The emergence of Delarivier (or "Mrs.") Manley, Mary Pix, and Catherine Trotter as dramatists in the next year called forth a brilliant and little-known travesty at Drury Lane—*The Female Wits* (1696). In the decade which followed, Susanna Centlivre began a long and ultimately distinguished career as a professional playwright. But her early struggles, her resorting to anonymity and even to the pretense of male gender, suggest that a full generation after the work of the first women writers reached the stage public resistance was still fierce.[41] Perhaps a few of the many anonymous plays from the late seventeenth century represent discreet female efforts. Most published plays identify the author, but not all. And in the theatre, most plays were mounted anonymously. Rumor might tout the appearance of a new show by Dryden

[41] See John Wilson Bowyer, *The Celebrated Mrs. Centlivre* (Durham, N.C.: Duke University Press, 1952), esp. pp. 47–48.

or Wycherley or Thomas Southerne, but not until 1699 was an author's name included on a playbill.[42] Obviously this state of affairs was conducive to the preservation of anonymity if a retiring young lady wished to be discreet.

Whoever "E. Polewheele" may have been, we have at the very least to grant that she wrote two quite professional plays at a date when female playwriting was almost unknown. She seems to have succeeded in getting at least one of them mounted professionally. Whether *The Frolicks* reached the stage or not—something we shall probably never know—we should remember that it is the first comedy written by a woman for professional production in England. To wonder what she might have been capable of had she gone on writing is idle speculation. But on the basis of her two youthful efforts, she must be accounted an impressively observant and ambitious pioneer.

[42] *The Letters of John Dryden*, ed. Charles E. Ward (1942; rpt. New York: AMS Press, 1965), #59.

TEXTUAL PRINCIPLES

Even by the freewheeling standards of other late seventeenth-century play manuscripts, the spelling and punctuation of *The Frolicks* are exceptionally idiosyncratic. No contemporary printer would have followed this copy closely. For the modern reader the quaintness of "ffor" and "mee" and "hayre" has charm, but "promistt'd," "he're," "couller," and "rouge" (rogue) can cause problems, and cumulatively hundreds of such cases pose a serious barrier to enjoyment, and even to comprehension. Therefore we have modernized the spelling, though we have tried to preserve the linguistic quality of the original by keeping changes to a minimum. Contractions have generally been retained. Thus "for's" and "see't" are preserved, while "detayn'd" is rendered as "detain'd" and "promistt'd" as "promis'd." Where spelling appears to be a key to special pronunciation—as with Zany, Sir Gregory, and their servants—we have altered it as little as possible. The manuscript is sparsely punctuated and eccentrically capitalized. Few speeches begin with a capital, and many have no terminal punctuation. We have simply followed modern conventions, though we have interpolated no more than the minimum of punctuation necessary for clarity. Where the author's punctuation makes the sense ambiguous we have given the literal manuscript reading in the Textual Notes. The syntax is frequently odd by present-day norms, but we have left it as is except in cases of apparent omission or error. Where substantive emendation is required the manuscript reading is given in the Textual Notes.

Two special problems in the manuscript are worthy of comment. The author occasionally encloses a few words in parentheses, usually foreshortened ones rather like inferior brackets. For example: "those that have ever seene ⌐my faythfull virgins⌐ and my Elysium." Exactly what she means by this we have not been able to discover. Our best guess is that these brackets represent a punctuation mark roughly equivalent to setting a phrase off in commas. Similar use of parentheses is to be found in the Ralph Crane transcripts. See W. W. Greg, "Some Notes on Crane's Manuscript of *The Witch*," *The Library*, 4th series, 22 (1942), 208–219, and *The Shakespeare First Folio* (1955), p. 100.

Even more mystifying is Polwhele's occasional use of a mark resembling a comma at the start of a line. This habit is displayed on twenty-seven pages, most of them in the first half of the manuscript. Sometimes a single, isolated line is so prefaced:

> you both must think
> my absence verry rude
> ,butt I have Aded to my
> ‚ house a drawing Roome . . .   [54r]

Usually no more than two or three scattered lines on a page are so distinguished, though in one instance ten consecutive lines were marked. A similar symbol is sometimes used in manuscripts or printed texts to show that a passage is quoted, or in play texts to indicate that it was omitted in performance. Neither could be the case here, especially as the material set off is not complete sentences. We have discerned no significance or pattern in these marks.

Certain points of policy should be noted. The names of the speakers are spelled out in full, and are regularized to the commonest form or a modern spelling in the speech tags. All abbreviations (for example, "Lad^sp:") are expanded. Foreign words and phrases have been put in italics. All quotation marks are editorial interpolations. Stage directions have been placed as seems appropriate to speech and action, not automatically positioned as they appear in the manuscript. Missed entrances, exits, and other stage directions have been added as necessary. Such additions have been placed in

brackets to distinguish them from the author's stage directions—thus [Exit. instead of (Exit. The author is entirely inconsistent in her use of Exit and Exeunt, and also in specifying who leaves when there can be any doubt. We have
silently regularized on these points. Similarly when the
manuscript reads "Enter lord and . . ." we have felt free to
specify the character's name, and we have followed a similar
policy on asides. The acts of the play comprise numerous
short, unnumbered scenes. When the setting definitely shifts
between scenes we have divided them with a printer's ornament. When a setting (in a street, for example) remains
unchanged we have indicated this in a note.

The Textual Notes at the back give the manuscript reading
in all instances where substantive emendation or correction
has been required. They also record cancellations, scribal
corrections, and so forth. Nine major varieties of problems
are involved. (1) Editorial emendations for sense or grammar.
(2) Cancellations and scribal blots. Where possible we have
reported the word or letters scribbled out. (3) Hiatuses in the
manuscript. In a few instances cropping or damage to the
manuscript has forced us to supply a word or phrase. We
have done so only when the sense demands it and the meaning of the passage is beyond reasonable doubt. (4) The
scribe's peculiar use of inferior brackets. There are seventy-
five instances of this device. Most appear meaningless, but
in some instances they may be a hint at the way a line was to
be delivered. (5) Carets. There are sixty-three instances of
careting in the manuscript. Thirty-three of them involve scribal cancellation and correction, and we have recorded all
such cases. Thirty involve nothing more than the filling-in of
a word momentarily omitted in copying; we have seen no
reason to record such cases. (6) Uncanceled repetitions of
words or phrases. (7) Doubtful words. (8) Instances where a
word has had to be supplied from the catchword. (9) Cropped
words. There are twenty-six instances of cropping. In only
eight of them can there be any doubt at all what the writer
meant. Consequently we have not entered cases like
believin[g] and interruptio[n] when the obvious conclusion

fits the context. As this list makes plain, we are dealing not with foul papers but with a rough fair copy in which the author felt free to make small verbal changes as she went along.

We have seen no point to recording the "prefatory comma" which recurs so frequently. Several specialists have been as baffled as we are by it, and it is illustrated in the second facsimile page for anyone curious about it. Likewise we have not recorded a frequent slip, *hin* for *him,* of which there are fourteen instances, one of them corrected by the author. Nor have we recorded the occasional use of tittles. There are twenty-three instances in the manuscript, but almost all of them are clearly nonfunctional. They usually occur in words which are not abbreviated (for example, anoth$\overline{\text{er}}$), and we can discern no scheme suggesting special or dialectal pronunciation. As L. C. Hector remarks in *The Handwriting of English Documents* (1966), "it would probably not be far wrong to describe as otiose any mark . . . which does not obviously replace letters necessary to the sense."

Principles of Annotation

Obsolete words and phrases are glossed at the bottom of each page. Glosses and explanatory notes are signaled by an asterisk (*) at the relevant point in the text. We have tried to be generous with glosses and explanations, though without the detail of the Revels Series. Many of the explanations will not be needed by Restoration drama specialists: our aim has been to make the play as readable as possible for the advanced student or the literate nonspecialist.

The Frolicks,

or The Lawyer Cheated.

A New Comedy, the
"First Copy"
Written by Mistress E. P.
1671

Present this.
humbly
To the Illustrious, and
most gracious Prince:
Prince Rupert.

Mighty prince:

          an vnfortunate younge
woman beggs she may not bee
more luckless in the presumption
of her dedication of a thing off
this nature, to your highness then
all others who are haunted with
Poetick diuills like mee: that
so disquiat vs we Canot find in
our hearts to let our Peters rest
(faime great Sir) has told mee your
grace is mercifull to those that
molest you with troubles of this

Leaf 2r (facsimile page)

Present this humbly
to the illustrious and
most gracious Prince,
Prince Rupert.*

Mighty Prince,

An unfortunate young woman begs she may not be more
luckless in the presumption of her dedication of a thing of
this nature to your Highness than all others who are haunted
with poetic devils like me—that so disquiet us we cannot find
in our hearts to let our betters rest. Fame, great sir, has told   10
me your grace is merciful to those that molest you with troubles of this nature. She farther adds you have a mind so
bright and glorious that it does not only light us poor admir-
ing mortals to adore you, but like the free and splendid eye of
heaven, the sun, ye with a gentle influence look and shine on
everything beneath you.* Encouraged much by Mistress
Fame I have for some minutes thrown my foolish modesty
aside, and with a boldness that does not well become a virgin,
presume to offer this comedy at your grace's feet, from
whence you may spurn it into nothing, if in anything it can   20
offend you. I dare not hope that there is ingenuity enough in
it to challenge much favor, but I must declare it is free from
abusing any person.* I question not but I shall be taxed for

Prince Rupert: Count Palatine of the Rhine and Duke of Bavaria, af-
terwards Duke of Cumberland and Earl of Holderness, 1619–1682. He was a
distinguished general, an influential member of the court of Charles II, and
a good friend of Thomas Killigrew (principal owner and manager of the
King's Company). See the Introduction.
    sun . . . you: This rhetorical extravagance is typical of such dedications.
Addressing the Earl of Orrery in *The Rival Ladies* (1664), Dryden said "the
Souls of other Men shine out at little Cranies; they understand some one
thing . . . while they are Darkned on all the other Parts: But your Lordship's
Soul is an intire Globe of Light, breaking out on every Side."
    abusing any person: In the late 1660s and early 1670s several plays had
appeared in which members of London society were satirically "personated."
Shadwell's *Sullen Lovers* (1668), the Howard and Buckingham *Country
Gentleman* (1669), and Buckingham's *Rehearsal* (1671) are famous instances. Shadwell's second original play, *The Humorists* (December 1670),
was allowed on stage only after the censor enforced radical changes. Dis-
claimers of personal satire were frequent in these years.

writing a play so comical, but those that have ever seen my *Faithful Virgins* and my *Elysium* * will justify me a little for writing this. I am young, no scholar, and what I write I write by nature, not by art. My careless stars so heedlessly do guide me as if they were unconcern'd with me, and my affairs lead me to nothing that is fortunate. But I shall grow incapable of misery, forget all their indifferent usage of me, and think that   30 they oblige me above all I can ever merit from them, if on this hour they'll be so kind to smile, in which I implore your Highness' pardon for my unparallel'd boldness, as I am a woman, and your protection for this comedy, to whom I humbly dedicate and commit it, who am a true honorer of your Highness' virtues, and your most luckless but devoted servant,

E. Polewheele

Faithful Virgins . . . Elysium: For a discussion of Polwhele's tragedy (extant as Bodleian MS. Rawl. Poet. 195), see the Introduction. We are unable to identify her *Elysium,* but the title sounds appropriate to a religious masque.

PERSONS*

Men

RIGHTWIT. An extravagant rake, bankrupt and hounded by cast mistresses demanding support for his numerous bastards. He falls in love with Clarabell and outwits her father to win her.

PHILARIO. Rightwit's bosom friend, and Clarabell's cousin. A hard-drinking, high-spirited young scapegrace.

SIR WILLIAM MEANWELL. A well-bred country knight, recently married in middle age to a young wife, whom he is determined to believe virtuous.

RALPH. Meanwell's servant, determined to make his reluctant master see the truth about his wife.

LORD COURTALL. A scheming, married gallant who seduces Mistress Faith and then maliciously tricks Frank Makelovè into marrying her for an imaginary fortune.

SIR FRANCIS MAKELOVE. A young man-about-town who pays court to Lady Meanwell and jumps at the chance to marry her sister Faith.

SWALLOW. A rich old lawyer, moneylender, and J.P. Father of Clarabell, and anxious to see her well married. A puritan 'cit'; testy but good-hearted.

MARK. Swallow's middle-aged clerk. A lover of wine, women, and song, who enjoys aiding and abetting Clarabell's schemes.

SIR GREGORY. A nouveau-riche young country knight, a hapless gull, come to town to find a wife.

Persons: Character descriptions and the list of minor parts have been supplied by the editors. See the Textual Notes.

MR. ZANY. A rich, silly, ill-bred heir from the country, come to town in search of a wife.

SPEAK. Sour-tempered country servant to Sir Gregory. Openly contemptuous of his young master.

PLAINMAN. Blunt-spoken country servant to Mr. Zany, whom he treats with half-affectionate contempt.

TURNKEY. A devout puritan.

PAGE to the Meanwells; SERVANTS attending the Meanwells; A GALLANT; PAGE to Lord Courtall; TWO DRAWERS; MUSICIANS; FIDDLERS; CONSTABLE; MESSENGER; SEDAN CHAIR CARRIERS; Six PAGES, TORCHBEARERS, and GALLANTS at a masked ball.

Women

CLARABELL. Swallow's daughter: wild, witty, beautiful, and self-willed. She falls in love with Rightwit.

LADY MEANWELL. A recently married country innocent who quickly learns the ways of London.

FAITH. Her sister, seduced by Lord Courtall but safely married off to Makelove under false pretences.

LEONORA. Rightwit's sister: beautiful, sober, virtuous.

PROCREATE. A French bawd, getting on in years and anxious to find a young, well-to-do husband.

MISTRESS of a Tavern.

Three WOMEN, cast mistresses of Rightwit.

ACT THE FIRST

Enter RIGHTWIT *and* LEONORA, *his sister.**

LEONORA. You were never virtuous—

RIGHTWIT. Why, what? Thou wilt not talk of virtue and be an ass? A thing no one so much as thinks on in this age, that is wise; more out of fashion than a French hood; and put on only by some old, moaded,* piteous souls that are not fit for anything but to count *Aves* on their beads to keep themselves from sleeping.

LEONORA. You are a precious gallant.

RIGHTWIT. You are a precious fool. Oh, those eyes of thine! Why should'st thou let * their storms thus, and about   10 their glorious sun cast a pall; * those taking light might * carry flame enough in them to kindle love's most furious fires in breasts more frozen than old age or charity.* Nay, let me gaze at thee——why, thou may'st make a mistress for a lord, and by thy noble trading redeem my almost lost estate again and make us a new fortune.

LEONORA. Dissemble goodness, if you have it not, and do not seem to the world's scan so wicked as you are. Re-

---

Enter . . . : The setting, unspecified, is the London lodging of Rightwit and Leonora, who are hosts to their kinsman Sir William Meanwell and his young wife, up from the country.

moaded: not in the *OED.* Presumably "outmoded" is meant.

let: hinder, obstruct.

cast a pall; might: We have supplied these words to make sense of the passage. Parts of the first page are damaged and illegible. For a discussion see the Textual Notes.

charity: Why charity is equated with old age, or "frozen," we cannot say. Rightwit is evidently making a snide remark.

member whom you have beneath your roof: your near
and worthy kinsman, Sir William Meanwell. Let not him   20
be a witness of your vices nor give him cause to think
you have a soul so black as to infect my white unblem-
ish'd thoughts with the least stain of its ill color.

RIGHTWIT. Let me clasp thee in my arms. I love thy virtue
dearly as my soul. I must abroad.

LEONORA. You still are sick of home. What? All the money
which ye last received is gone, of a hundred pound y'ave
not one penny left in ten days' space.

RIGHTWIT. Thou liest: here's eight shillings. The rest indeed
is all confounded; wine and women must be had, Nell.   30
Besides there is a law that says—

LEONORA. What?

RIGHTWIT. That children must not be knock'd i'th' head, and
those that get them must keep them.

LEONORA. Why do not you marry?

RIGHTWIT. I have a good reason for't; that is, I cannot tie
myself to love one woman; no more than your fantastic *
can tie himself to one mode. Farewell.

LEONORA. When will you return?

RIGHTWIT. What an idle question's that?   (Exit.   40

LEONORA. There is no talking to him—   (Exit.

▼

A table discovered.* SIR WILLIAM MEANWELL and his LADY at
supper, with servants attending. LADY offers to rise. He
stays her.

MEANWELL. Why do you rise so oft, and run to the balcony
and smile, and gaze at me at your return? You shall not
stir again till I am satisfied.

LADY MEANWELL. There is no Elysium but this London.
Without question, it is the lovers' Heaven.

MEANWELL. This is from the purpose—

    fantastic: a man given to fine or showy dress; a fop.
    discovered: The shutters draw aside to expose action in progress. The set-
ting is another room in Rightwit's lodging.

LADY MEANWELL. What wretched fools are those that forsake
this soul-charming city for the dirty, melancholy country.*   50
MEANWELL. Why dost thou fix thy eyes so steadfastly upon
me, ha?
LADY MEANWELL. Methoughts you were the handsom'st man
in the country—but here there are so many that excel
you, that now in my opinion you are nobody.
MEANWELL. Thou speakest with such an innocent freeness
that what thou say'st is not of force to make me jealous,
or I should envy all that you so think excel me.
LADY MEANWELL. Nay, now let me go again.
MEANWELL. Take your swing.   60
[Aside] I must get her away; if these kind of crotchets
come in her head, mine may chance ache for't.* But she
is young and free from guile, or else she better might
disguise her thoughts (as many a cunning gipsy would),
if she meant mischief.
                                        (Exeunt.
                        (The servants take up the table.)

Enter SIR FRANCIS MAKELOVE and MADAM PROCREATE.

PROCREATE. Is my lady in her lodgin's, page?
PAGE. She is in the drawing room. I will acquaint her of your
being here.   [Exit.

Enter LADY MEANWELL.

LADY MEANWELL. Your most humble servant.
PROCREATE. Noblest lady, yours. Here is a worthy friend of   70
mine, ambitious to present his service to your ladyship.
LADY MEANWELL. I shall esteem myself much honored,
madam, in the knowledge of any of your friends.

country: an example of the town-country dichotomy which is a commonplace in Restoration comedy. Contempt for the boring, rustic, ungenteel
life outside of London is so nearly universal in these plays that to find the attitude reversed, as in The Country Gentleman or in some Shadwell plays,
comes as a shock.
  ache for't: i.e., she will cuckold him.

(MAKELOVE *kisses the lady's hands.*) Page, give us some
  seats. [PAGE *provides chairs.*] Will you please to sit?

PROCREATE. I was in no little fear this glorious evening had
  'ticed you abroad. It is most sweet weather.

MAKELOVE. It is, much. It does not invite your ladyship to
  take it in Gray's Inn Walks, or Hyde Park? *

LADY MEANWELL. I have seen none of these places since I   80
  came to town, nor know not where they are.

MAKELOVE. Will you vouchsafe me the blessing to wait upon
  you to them?

LADY MEANWELL. I know not how to merit so great a favor
  from you, sir.

PROCREATE [*aside*]. So, he is enter'd now; I'll leave them.
  [*To Lady Meanwell*] Where is Sir William, madam?

LADY MEANWELL. Very busy in the drawing room with an old
  romance, which he takes more delight in than praying.

MAKELOVE [*aside*]. She is fair and airy. These French people   90
  are ingenious, and please in everything they do for us.

PROCREATE. Madam, shall I not be too unmannerly to inter-
  rupt his meditations?

LADY MEANWELL. No, no. You will find him in the next
  room. Pray, please to visit him.

PROCREATE. *Très homble serviteur, mademoiselle.*   [*Exit.*

LADY MEANWELL. I should not believe this lady were of
  France, she speaks English so admirably, but that I am
  by some friends satisfied that she is of that nation.*

Gray's Inn Walks . . . Hyde Park: Gray's Inn (one of the Inns of Court,
not a tavern) is located near the head of Chancery Lane between High Hol-
born and what is now Theobald's Road. Of it Strype observes that the "chief
Ornament belonging to this Inn, is its spacious Garden, with curious Walks,
as well as those that are shady by the lofty Trees, as those that are raised
higher, and lie open to the Air, and the enjoyment of a delightful prospect of
the Fields. And this Garden hath been, for many Years, much resorted unto,
by the Gentry of both Sexes" (*A Survey of the Cities of London and Westminster,* by John Stow, corrected and enlarged by John Strype, 6 pts. in 2
vols. [London: A. Churchill, 1720], pt. 3, pp. 253–254). "Hyde Park," a royal
hunting preserve in the time of Henry VIII and a racecourse in the reign of
Charles I, had by this time become a popular promenade and drive at the
western end of the city.

    that nation: French women had a reputation for lasciviousness and sexual
intrigue.

MAKELOVE. She is most perfect in our language. But madam,   100
    shall I have the honor to carry you to the park, and
    thence to see an excellent new play at court * tonight?

LADY MEANWELL. The honor will be mine, in having your
    noble company. But I must not tantalize myself with
    seeing pleasures I must be snatched from ere I can
    enjoy them. Mr. Meanwell had rather hear the cuckoo
    sing in his own manor, than all those heavenly choir
    that chant the divine lays in Westminster Abbey, and
    swears a mummery or morris dance perform'd by his
    hinds * at home is beyond all the plays at both houses.*   110

MAKELOVE. What an erroneous opinion is this in him! We
    must use some charm to convert him.

LADY MEANWELL. He perfectly hates London, and is unalter-
    ably resolved to leave it next week.

MAKELOVE. Madam, there will soon be a faction against Sir
    William, if he go about to rob us of you so quickly, that
    have so short a moment enrich'd us with your presence
    here at town. Faith, please to let me wait of you to take
    the air—and by the way we will design how we shall
    make him alter this severe resolve.   120

LADY MEANWELL. It is beyond the reach of wit.

To them SIR WILLIAM MEANWELL *and* PROCREATE.

LADY MEANWELL. Sir, here is a worthy person would will-
    ingly be known to you.

at court: Plays were frequently staged at the court theatre in Whitehall by
the two regular London companies and occasionally by visiting foreign trou-
pes. Such performances occasioned much fancy dress and social display, and
they were usually available gratis to the gentry. On this subject see Eleanore
Boswell, *The Restoration Court Stage* (1932).

mummery . . . morris dance . . . hinds: A mummery is a dumb show. A
morris dance is a mumming in fancy costume featuring extravagant dancing. Characters from the Robin Hood legend were often portrayed. It is a
decidedly rustic entertainment. Hinds are servants, or in this context farm
laborers.

both houses: the two professional theatres in London. The King's Company occupied a building in Bridges Street; the Duke's Company moved
from Lincoln's Inn Fields to its elegant new Dorset Garden theatre in November 1671.

MAKELOVE. It is the greatest of my ambition.

MEANWELL. I shall be proud of your acquaintance.

PROCREATE. Will your ladyship to the park and breathe a little fresh air?

LADY MEANWELL. With all my heart. I am almost stifled. Page, see my coach ready at the door.   [*Exit* PAGE. [*To Meanwell*] Dear mine, I will not ravish you from the   130 sweet consolation you find in the old romances (which I know you value above the town pleasures), but commit you to divert yourself with Guy of Warwick, Montelion, and the brave achievements of the Knight of the Sun * and the rest of those excellent heroes which you delight in—and expect an account of their enterprises at my return from you.

MEANWELL. Give me leave to see you coach'd.*

MAKELOVE. I beseech you give me leave to wait upon my lady.   140

PROCREATE. By no means, Sir William, will I take you from your study. I will follow my lady. Your most humble servant.   (*Exeunt omnes. Manet* MEANWELL.

MEANWELL. They oblige me to stay at home, spite of my heart. And I must take it for a courtesy that my wife goes abroad with a gallant, a man *à la mode,* to wait on her in my place, I know not whither nor to do what. I was bewitch'd to bring her to London; but yet there may be no harm in all this.   (*Exit.*

▼

Guy of Warwick, Montelion, and . . . the Knight of the Sun: *Guy of Warwick* is a popular chivalric romance (ca. 1300). Montelion is the protagonist of Emanuel Foord's popular *The Famous Historie of Montelyon, Knight of the Oracle* (1633, and many times reprinted). The name was used as a pseudonym by John Phillips in his *Don Juan Lamberto: Or, a Comical History of the Late Times,* "By Montelion Knight of the Oracle" (1661), but we can discern no reference to Phillips' topical satire. "The Knight of the Sun" is the hero of the romance *Caballero del Febo, Espejo de Principes y Caballeros,* by Diego Ortuñez de Calahorra and Marcos Martínez, first printed at Saragossa in 1562, and mentioned prominently in *Don Quixote.*

coach'd: provided with a coach. Since this is their own, he is merely seeing her to the coach.

Enter LORD COURTALL *and a* GALLANT.*

COURTALL. Was not that Frank Makelove we saw pass by   150
　with the handsome lady in the fine new coach? With the
　French mademoiselle just now?

GALLANT. It was, my lord.

COURTALL. A plague of that French *crapaud.** May the
　scourge of her own nation light upon her: that is, the
　pox.

GALLANT. She has dishumor'd your lordship?

COURTALL. Yes. Fare you well—　　　　(*Exit* COURTALL.

GALLANT. The hotspot* smarts and burns sure—which
　makes his lordship so pettish. The French woman   160
　should have apply'd a remedy and has fail'd. 'Tis that
　makes him wince and, a thousand to one, will compel
　him to kick Makelove for getting the cure before him.
　　　　　　　　　　　　　　　　(*Exit* GALLANT.

Enter at one door SIR GREGORY, *at the other* MR. ZANY, *with
their two men,* SPEAK *and* PLAINMAN.*

ZANY. Sir Gregory, your servant.

SIR GREGORY. Dear Zany. And what in troth make you in
　town?

ZANY. I scarce know myself, but my uncle sent for me; I
　must be married with all speed, man. His sending for me
　was to motion me to a wife.

SIR GREGORY. No doubt but she has money enough, if he   170
　have a finger i'th' pie. But has she any beauty?

ZANY. No matter for beauty. There are pretty wenches enow
　in London and at easy rates, if a man have money.

PLAINMAN. Aye, and pocky whores, too—

Enter . . . : the street.
crapaud: French for "toad."
　hotspot: The gallant implies that Courtall is made irritable by the symp-
toms of venereal disease—but also suggests that the "cure" he desires is a
chance of bedding Procreate's new protégée.
Enter . . . : The scene continues in the street.

ZANY. You saucy cur, I must muzzle you. You will still be shaming my discourse with one rude phrase or other.

PLAINMAN. Thy father would not have us'd me so. God's nownes,* I think thou art a very bastard.

ZANY. You'll ha' done.

PLAINMAN. Mum.   180

SIR GREGORY. Nay, I am going a-wiving too, dear Zany. Let me have thy company to my mistress.

SPEAK. Ah, that you're a great loggerhead. Such another word and, by Gud, I'll swinge * you.

ZANY. Where lives your lady, noble Sir Gregory?

SIR GREGORY. At— at— at— (*His man stops his mouth.*) The devilish rogue will querken * me. I'll see you at your lodgin'.

ZANY. Where may I wait of you at yours?

SIR GREGORY. Shall I tell him, Speak?   190

SPEAK. Tell a fool's head.*

SIR GREGORY. Faith, I can't think o'th' name on't, but it is between Temple Bar and Westminster.*

PLAINMAN. You might have told a wise man so and kept yourself a fool still.

SIR GREGORY. I know the way to't as straight as a line, but have forgot its title, as the gallants phrase it. But where may I find you?

SPEAK. Amongst the common bawdy places, any day.

ZANY. That might have been kept in, you rascal.   200

God's nownes: probably "God save his own," although it could be a deformation of "God's wounds."

swinge: beat or flog.

querken: choke, strangle.

a fool's head: a head void of sense or intelligence; a foolish person.

Temple Bar and Westminster: "Temple Bar" is "the Place where the Freedom of the City of *London,* and the Liberty of the City of *Westminster* doth part." Located on the Strand about three blocks from the supposed site of Procreate's house, it was originally a timber building standing in the road, but "since the great Fire, there is erected a stately Gate, with two Posterns, on each side, for the Convenience of Foot Passengers; with strong Gates to shut up in the Nights" (Strype's Stow, pt. 3, p. 278). "Westminster," long the site of the King's principal palace and later of several courts and the Houses of Parliament, is well over a mile away, so Sir Gregory's explanation is fatuously unhelpful.

SIR GREGORY. Well, Mr. Zany, lose no time. I'll to my
     mistress—
ZANY. Good luck attend you, dear Sir Gregory—I'll take your
     counsel.   (*Exeunt severally.*

Enter RIGHTWIT *and* SWALLOW.*

RIGHTWIT. You know my business. I want money.
SWALLOW. Pray let me be quiet. You have already had much
     more than I shall ere have satisfaction for. Your land's
     not worth the sum I have already lent you, nor have I
     more for you.   (*Exit* SWALLOW.
RIGHTWIT. The rogue answers me as if I begg'd an alms. Oh,   210
     how I could rail and chafe and curse now. But the vil-
     lain's got out o'th' hearing on't. I'll follow, and kick him
     into honesty.   (*Exit.

▼

Enter SWALLOW, *his daughter* CLARABELL, *and* MARK, *his
clerk.**

SWALLOW. Clarabell, the greatest of my ambition is to see
     you happy in the arms of a husband that may please you.
CLARABELL. I would not have one do displease me.
SWALLOW. Will you give me leave to choose one for you?
CLARABELL. No, never, sir.
SWALLOW. How!
CLARABELL. You shall please to take leave.   220
SWALLOW. Very well. What say you to the alderman's son?
     Could you not like him well, ha?
CLARABELL. Admirably, for a fool in a morris dance.
SWALLOW. A fool! Thou rascal.
CLARABELL. Be not offended, sir. The old proverb says he that
     acts the fool is the most ingenious of the company.* I
     like his wit.

Enter Rightwit . . . : The scene continues in the street.
Enter Swallow . . . : Swallow's office.
     he that acts . . . : evidently a mock-proverb, concocted on the spot by
Clarabell.

SWALLOW. Or will you needs be a lady? What say you to the country knight? Will you have him?

CLARABELL. Yes, when I am weary of my life.   230

SWALLOW. Weary of thy life, harlot?

CLARABELL. My single life, I mean, sir.

MARK (*aside*). A good wench.

SWALLOW. That you soon will be. Let me see. The judge's son hath a month's mind of you.* Your opinion of him?

CLARABELL. I like him past expression for the most part; he plays the idiot with a grace, and seems an arrant puppy naturally.

SWALLOW. Out of my sight!

CLARABELL. You'll not be angry for saying he behaves himself 240 *à la mode*? 'Tis the fashion to play the fool, and much they are cry'd up that do it handsomely.

MARK (*aside*). Rare—he's pacified again.

SWALLOW. I'll compel you to nothing. But finding you indifferent to all I've mention'd yet, if I might advise you, you should take one that is old, wise, and rich—my Brother Joseph *—shall I chop up a bargain * between you?

CLARABELL. I confess he has wealth enough to spare a young wife to purchase a stately pair of horns of what gallant she pleases; wise enough to make an apology for wear- 250 ing them; and old enough, of all conscience, to become them excellently.

SWALLOW. Nay, now I perceive thou art a carrion; * get you in, you slut.

[*Aside*] This wench is knavish; very full of knavery.

[*To Clarabell*] Come again here, jewel. How dar'st thou thus palpably abuse thy own natural father?

---

month's mind: an inclination, fancy, liking for. In English rustic tradition the "month's mind" is a celebration held one month from the date of a funeral. Hence Swallow may be implying that the young man, celebrating a recent inheritance, has taken a sudden fancy to Clarabell, though the phrase may have lost this associative meaning by 1671.

Brother Joseph: a fellow member of Swallow's dissenting sect.

chop up a bargain: to barter keenly for a good deal.

carrion: rotten, vile, loathsome, disgusting (obsolete figurative usage from "corpse").

a husband that may please you.

Clar. J would not haue one do displease me.

Swd. will you giue mee leaue
to choose one for you.

Clar. no neuer sir.

Swd. how!

Clar. you shall please to take leaue.

Swd. verry well; what say you to
the Alderman's sonne, could you
not like him well ha?

Clar. , Admirably; for a foole in a
, morris dance.

Swd. a foole; thou rascall.

Clar. , (be not offended sir) the old
, prouerb says he that act's the
, foole is the most ingenious of
the Company, J like his witt
or will you needs be a Lady
what say you to the Country
knight, will you haue him

Clar. yes, when J am weary of my
life ——

Swd.

CLARABELL. Lord, sir, I thought you had but jested when you
    talked of "chopping me in marriage," as you call it, with
    an old man, and my answer was to make you merry. But   260
    since you are in earnest, I humbly beg your pardon.
SWALLOW. Beg my pardon—pray God thou art not naught,*
    thou comest off and on with so many plaguy fetches *
    and "why not's" that I am very 'fraid on thee. "Practice
    not deceit in thy youth." *
MARK (*aside*). You'll deceive him—
CLARABELL (*aside*). If I can, by my troth.   (*Exeunt.*

[End of Act I]

naught: immoral, wicked.
fetches: dodges, tricks.
Practice not deceit . . .: spoken as a proverb, though the expression does
not appear in the usual proverb dictionaries.

ACT THE SECOND

Enter RIGHTWIT *as to a door. He knocks.**

CLARABELL (*within*). Who's there?
RIGHTWIT. A man.
CLARABELL. How should I know that?
RIGHTWIT. Appear, and I will satisfy thee.
CLARABELL. As I live, a handsome fellow. I must prate with
    him.

Enter CLARABELL.

    Now sir; your business.
RIGHTWIT. You shall dispatch it, if you please.
CLARABELL. Why, so I will, if that be all. I pray be gone; the
    door gapes to swallow you. Will you exit?   10
RIGHTWIT [*aside*]. How she smirks and simpers.
    [*To Clarabell*] Pretty, airy rascal, I cannot for my heart
    leave thee yet. Prithee, what art?
CLARABELL. A maid.
RIGHTWIT. 'Tis pity thou should'st be one. Let me make thee
    other—
CLARABELL. I am not at my last prayer yet, to cry "come any,
    good Lord, any." *
RIGHTWIT. Thou art no kin to the fellow of this house, cer-
    tainly.   20

    Enter . . . : Swallow's office.
my last prayer . . . "come any, good Lord any": Proverbial cry of the old
maid, praying for any husband in order to avoid leading apes in Hell. Cf.
Southerne's *The Maid's Last Prayer, or Any Rather than Fail* (1693).

73

CLARABELL. Very right. He is neither my uncle nor cousin, but even my "own natural father," as he terms it.

RIGHTWIT. The pox he is. Why, he never got * a hair of thee.

CLARABELL. No, he got me all, sir, all.

RIGHTWIT. The devil 'a did. Was thy mother handsome?

CLARABELL. The original copy of me.

RIGHTWIT. Without question then, thou had'st some other father than the merely suppos'd Swallow.

CLARABELL. You'll go near to make me a bastard presently. *Adieu*—   30

RIGHTWIT. Nay, we must not part yet. Thy very eyes tell me thou wilt stay a little longer. I must needs kiss thee.

CLARABELL. You will not offer it.

RIGHTWIT. Then would you laugh at me? But I'll give you no cause.

(Kisses her.)

Thy skin's pure, teeth white, lips soft, breath sweet, eyes sparkling. Would we were in a wilderness together.

CLARABELL [*breaks away*]. You dare as well be hang'd as serve me so again, you saucy—

RIGHTWIT. Oh, excellent. Dost thou dare me to it? Well, once   40 more you shall see what I dare do, then.

(Kisses her again. She shrieks.)

Dost cry out for more?

(Kisses her again.)

CLARABELL [*breaks away*]. Get out.

RIGHTWIT. Thou makest a dog on me.* Have a care I do not fasten on thee. Wilt thou be kind * a little and—

CLARABELL. Do what?

RIGHTWIT. That as is in fashion most, and ever was, since first the world began. If thou know'st not the mode, lead me to thy bed and I will teach it thee and make thee perfect in the fashion. Dost understand me?   50

got: begot, fathered.

makest a dog on . . . fasten on: To "make a dog" is to make a decisive choice—too hastily, Rightwit implies here, adding an obscene suggestion of his own.

be kind: euphemism for sexually compliant.

CLARABELL. Partly—but before you are my schoolmaster, pray let me know you a little better. What's your name?

RIGHTWIT. My name and nature are no kin. "Rightwit" men call me—but thy father knows I am a fool.

CLARABELL. So does his daughter too, if you be he. Did you not chaffer * away a brave * estate for wine, pox, and wenches? Precious merchandise!

RIGHTWIT. Pretty, abusive devil.

CLARABELL. My father will provide me another bedfellow, I assure you, to teach me the mode you talk of. However   60
I'll cross myself when I but hear you named.*

RIGHTWIT. Hang me if I love thee not, past sense and reason, although thy father is a cutthroat rascal, who gulls such addle-brain'd puppies out of their estates, as I am, and formally covers all his roguery with a damn'd cloak of law. My business hither was to curse him to his great master, the Devil, before he should by bargain and the statute of Hell fetch him. But for thy sake I'll now forbear.

CLARABELL. Peace, issue of a nightmare, abusive fiend.   70

Enter MARK.

CLARABELL. How now?

MARK. A couple of country wooers within desire to have audience for a little discourse of love, mistress.   [*Exit.*

CLARABELL. You will leave me to my business now, I hope.

RIGHTWIT. No, I will stay and hear what the country men can say for themselves.

CLARABELL. I won't be wooed in public.

RIGHTWIT. Then will I woo thee myself in private.

CLARABELL. I think I shall have much ado to be shut of you.

chaffer: exchange, barter.

brave: "an indeterminate word, used to express the superabundance of any valuable quality" (*OED*).

cross myself . . . : Clarabell implies that Rightwit is a demon whose influence must be warded off with the sign of the cross.

Well, since there's no remedy—Mark, bid them ap-   80
proach.

Enter MARK *with* SIR GREGORY *and* ZANY *with their men,*
SPEAK *and* PLAINMAN.

SPEAK [*to Plainman*]. Why how now! Pray, come back. My
master is a knight. Give your betters place, since you
both have 'casion here.

PLAINMAN. God's nownes! Thy master's grandsire was a
nailer. His knighthood came out of the nail bag, did it
not, thou son of a fanatic? *

SPEAK. Spawn of a toad, thou liest, and thy lie savors worse
than the garbage of the Devil.

PLAINMAN. Give me the lie? By Gud I'll send my tyke dog *   90
about thy ears.

(*They fight.* ZANY *and the* KNIGHT *go to part them, and they
set upon their masters.*)

SIR GREGORY. God'so,* Mr. Zany, shift for yourself. The
knaves will baffle us. Murder! Murder!
                    (*Exeunt* SIR GREGORY *and* MR. ZANY.
                    (RIGHTWIT *and* CLARABELL *laugh.*)

PLAINMAN. God's nownes, you hobbyhorses. What is't you
laugh at? Can you tell?

SPEAK. Are yo' the gentlewoman my master should woo?

CLARABELL. So they say.

SPEAK. By my troth, he shall ha' none o' you by my consent.
You do so fleer and gibber * that I dare swear you are not

fanatic: literally, an unreasoning enthusiast. Applied to nonconformists in
the latter half of the seventeenth century as a hostile epithet.

tyke dog: a mongrel. The phrase is often used with an implied connection
to Yorkshire, where tyke was once the word for dog.

God'so: variant of *Gadso* (from oaths beginning "God's") and *catso* (from
the Italian), which comingled during the seventeenth century. In this context it is an exclamation of reproach or alarm without particular meaning.

fleer and gibber: laugh and chatter contemptuously.

so honest as you should be. Besides you look no more   100
like a maid, than I look like an emparoll *— (*They laugh.*)
RIGHTWIT. I hope he touch'd your copyhold there.*
CLARABELL. He is an ass, and you are another.
   [*To Plainman*] Sirrha, shall I have thy consent to marry
   with thy master?
PLAINMAN. As you two can 'gree. But to be downright, I like
   not such a young fizgig * cockney; * you none of you are
   good for ought but to breed a generation of beggars on.
   You cannot winnow, I warrant, nor know what belongs
   to serving any sow but yourself.*   110
RIGHTWIT. A shrewd, blunt clown. I think I must take thee
   out of pity, for fear thou lead'st apes in Hell.
CLARABELL. No, I'll rather go thither with my monkeys with a
   hope to meet you there with your bears, my jackanapes,*
   and they will make all the devils in Hell sport, and we
   shall have a merry Eternity on't.
RIGHTWIT. I have none to bring there. I lost my bachelorship
   so long ago that I defy the name of one. But if all bache-
   lors must lead bears and all maids apes in Hell, thou and
   I shall both go to Heaven, since thou art sure no more a   120
   maid than I a bachelor.*

emparoll: evidently a deformation of "emperor."
copyhold: claim to possession (usually of land, figuratively of other things) based on lengthy tenure. For estates, this could be demonstrated by rent-rolls from "time immemorial." Speak says Clarabell's pert ways are inconsistent with virginity; Rightwit chimes in to suggest that she has no proof of the status she claims.
fizgig: a light, frivolous woman, fond of gadding about.
cockney: a bantering or contemptuous name for a born Londoner. In the seventeenth century the term was occasionally applied to a wanton or affected woman. More commonly, it served as a derisive appellation for a townsman in contrast to the hardier inhabitants of the country. The OED cites B.E.'s *Dictionary of the Canting Crew* (ca. 1690) under cockney: "one ignorant in Country Matters." Plainman's belief in the importance of agricultural expertise would of course appear comic to the London audience.
You cannot winnow . . . . : She is a city girl with no farming skills.
jackanapes: an impertinent fellow, one who assumes ridiculous airs.
bachelor: evidently used here to mean a male virgin. The OED does not cite such a usage, though the term may mean "beginner" or "novice." Cf. W. S. Gilbert's line in *The Gondoliers:* "she's *not* a beginner."

CLARABELL. You say, and unsay. Talk not another word to me.

[*To the servants*] Where are your masters?

PLAINMAN. Mine's at one bawdy place or other, I dare swear. He's devilish lecherous. I must go hunt him out. (*Exit.*

SPEAK. Mine rambles amongst the ballad singers and puppet players, where the rogues pick his pocket *probatum.** And yet the oaf will not take warning. By Gud, I'll flounce * him. By your leave—   (*Exit.*   130

CLARABELL. This fellow has some manners.

RIGHTWIT. The sport * is at the best. I'll leave thee too—

CLARABELL. You speak against your conscience now. You had as lief be hang'd, I know, as go yet. But there is the door—

Enter SIR GREGORY *and* ZANY *again.*

RIGHTWIT. The lovers re-enter. Now I will not hence yet.

CLARABELL. If you have no business here but laughing, you shall not stay.

RIGHTWIT. Nay, I will find other business, if thou wilt. But oh! for a sentence—there is one a-coming out of the   140 knight's mouth.*

SIR GREGORY. Mistress, I should have address'd myself to you before, but I have such a son of Belial to my man, I dare say nothing as I would sometimes for him. In plain country terms, I will, if you please, make you a lady.

CLARABELL. My knight comes to the point.

ZANY. Give one leave to speak, as has not spoke yet. I can

---

probatum: Latin *probatum est,* "it has been proven." Speak is implying that this happens regularly.

flounce: to dash or drive with violence. Speak implies that he will shoo Sir Gregory back to safety.

The sport: amorous dalliance or diversion. Rightwit is saying that this is the time of day (or night) for picking up women.

knight's mouth: Sir Gregory is preparing to deliver a formal speech with a flourish. Rightwit's comment likens him to a figure in a broadside cartoon.

purchase a knighthood too.* His came out of the virtue
of sparables.*

SIR GREGORY. Sirrha,* thou dost well to cry "whore" first. Thy   150
father was a dog collar maker, was 'a not?

ZANY. Go look. Mistress, I have more mind to talk to you than
him. He is but an ass, for all he is a new-made knight.

CLARABELL. Nay, to 't again. I like your discourse admirably.
Ye warble rarely.

RIGHTWIT. Pretty rascal.

SIR GREGORY. What the Devil! Dost thou think to baffle me,
mistress? If you have more mind of him than of me, I
care not a farthing for you.

CLARABELL. I swear I love you equally.   160

SIR GREGORY. I love not to be baffled. Come farther, you im-
pudent puppy.*

ZANY. How many such had thy dam, ye coxcomb, at a litter?

SIR GREGORY. Now by my honor I'll fight thee, though I die in
the place, for this very affront, thou son of a she-devil.

[*They fight.*]

  purchase a knighthood: Technically, birth, merit, and estate were
required, but knighthood had lost much of its dignity during the seventeenth
century. James I expanded upon his predecessors' device of compelling
those who held "lands of a certain yearly value" to pay the fee to become
knights, or pay a fine for being exempted. Charles II discontinued the practice of forcing knighthood on possessors of "Knights' fees," but in 1671 any
man who came of age and was willing to spend enough money to "prove" his
birth and merit could "purchase" a knighthood. Money alone could make
one a knight bachelor: influence was required to gain entree into exclusive
fraternal orders like The Bath and The Garter. As late as 1842 the immediate
fee for registering knighthood amounted to only £108. All Zany need do is
pay a herald to draw up a respectable-looking genealogy and announce his
inheritance to the right tax collector. The title thus gained, however, was no
great distinction. See Sir Nicholas Harris Nicolas, *History of the Orders of
Knighthood of The British Empire*, I (London: John Hunter, 1842), esp. iii,
v, xvii, xviii, and xxx.
  sparables: small, headless, wedge-shaped iron nails used in the soles and
heels of boots and shoes.
  Sirrha: a familiar term of address to men or boys, usually expressing contempt, reprimand, or assumption of authority on the part of the speaker. The
origin and meaning of the second syllable are obscure.
  Come farther . . . puppy: Sir Gregory evidently pulls Zany away from
Clarabell.

Enter PHILARIO.

PHILARIO. How now? What's the matter?

CLARABELL. Pox on 'em. Part them. I love not these tragic comedies.*

RIGHTWIT. Hold, ye incomparable brace of coxcombs.

SIR GREGORY. I will have Mistress Swallow, in spite of this   170
rogue that hoped to baffle me.

ZANY. Rogue! In your heart you shall not have a hair of her.

RIGHTWIT. Ye neither of you shall have half a hair of her.
Dare but once more to think on her, and I will make you
forget the memory of all things but my feet, you unparal-
leled idiots.

SIR GREGORY. I have forgot her, sir, already. I—

ZANY. I can forget her too.

SIR GREGORY. A dish of sack will wash the remembrance of
her clearly out of my soul.   180
[*Aside to Rightwit*] But I would not that this codshead
should baffle me.

RIGHTWIT. Oh, admirable, Sir Gregory.

PHILARIO. Rightwit, a word. (*They whisper.*)

RIGHTWIT. Rare. It shall be so.

SIR GREGORY. Hang her, if she had loved me, she would have
scorned to have seen me abused after so horrid a nature.

RIGHTWIT. Gentlemen, let me compose the difference betwixt
you. Come, your hands so. [*Makes them shake hands.*]
This is well. 'Tis pity you should e'er be enemies, you are   190
so equally qualified. You'll excuse the unsoftness of my
temper. I am humourous as Woman, and can change as
often. Shall we try what the pow'r of wine can do towards
making me forget my debts and you your love? This
wench is proud, and ill-natured to boot. Or if you needs
must be amorous, I'll bring you to a mistress gentle as
Love himself, fresh as the youthful morn, and sweeter
than the breaths of roses be.

these tragic comedies: a derisive comment about swordplay comedies of
the Spanish-romance sort popular in the 1660s after the great success of
Tuke's *Adventures of Five Hours* (1663).

ZANY. March on.
SIR GREGORY. March on.   200
RIGHTWIT. Advance and follow me.
CLARABELL. A good riddance of ye all.
(*Exeunt* SIR GREGORY, ZANY *and* PHILARIO. RIGHTWIT *exits
smiling on* CLARABELL. *Manet* CLARABELL.

CLARABELL. There's witchcraft in everything this fellow
    does. My soul is ready to run out at my eyes after him. I
    fear I shall be fool enough, and madwoman together, to
    fall in love with him. But I will resist it with an Amazo-
    nian courage. Love is but a swinish thing at best. I'll in,
    and study to forget him. If 'twill not be, I'll study how to
    get him.   (*Exit.*

▼

Enter PROCREATE *at one door, at the other* LORD COURTALL.*

PROCREATE. *Très homble serviteur, mon seigneur.*   210
COURTALL. The Devil take your ladyship's French compli-
    ments and all your wicked bawdy tricks together.
PROCREATE. How have I merited this intolerable affront from
    you, my rude, mis-manner'd lord? You do not know me,
    sure.
COURTALL. But I do—for an exquisite and honorable pro-
    curer. You seldom bawd, I dare make answer for you, for
    any under the degree of a lord. But I perceive Sir Francis
    Makelove has tempted your venerable ladyship to break
    your old custom. For which you should, by my consent,   220
    trade no longer in that vocation for any of us. You will
    ere long be entreated by our grooms and footmen to do
    the office for them.
PROCREATE. These abuses are insupportable. I came with all
    the civility imaginable to invite you to my house tonight,
    which will be graced with such perfection as till now this
    town could never boast of—the excellent Lady Mean-

Enter . . . : Lord Courtall's lodgings.

well, and her beauteous sister who came but yesternight
to make it happy with her presence. But I shall spare my
invitation, and entreat your abusive honor to be less lav-   230
ish of your affronts. I shall find else a thousand friends of
France 'twixt Westminster and Temple Bar for to revenge me of your passionate and black mouth'd great-
ness.

COURTALL. Half that number, madam, might go near to worst
me. 'Tis good to compound with you. I have not in England and Wales the tithe o'th' friends your ladyship has
in a little mile. Here's twenty guineas.* Would you
please to bestow them in some handsome sweetmeats to
treat these beauteous miracles you speak of? And let me   240
by ocular vein * satisfy myself how well they like them.
You shall infinitely endear me to you, if to this happiness
you join your pardon for my late rudeness.

PROCREATE. Your lordship knows I'm of a soft and melting
nature, which does encourage you to use me any how.
At night you may expect to find a kind reception at my
house. Till when, I commit you to what you please.

(Exit.

COURTALL. I must leave drabbing * at these unreasonable
French rates. I shall be ruin'd else—all will sink. But this
I do to cross Makelove.   250
[Calls offstage.] Who's there?

Enter PAGE.

Go boy, bid Mountla * set my clothes out I wore to
Windsor.* I must to Court tonight.

twenty guineas: The guinea is an English gold coin, first struck in 1663 to
commemorate the chartering of the New Guinea Company. Its nominal
value was 20s. Guineas were somewhat scarce, and worth a premium, since
they were gold rather than silver. See Pepys, 29 October 1666. One cannot
give a precise equivalent in modern money, but a society playboy giving a
procurer $500 in hundred dollar bills may be a rough analogue.
ocular vein: i.e., by seeing for himself.
drabbing: whoring.
Mountla: evidently Lord Courtall's valet. No such character actually appears in the play. The derivation and significance of this peculiar name
remain obscure, but the manuscript reading is absolutely clear.
Windsor: Windsor Castle in Berkshire, some twenty miles west of London,

PAGE. Here is a gentleman with letters waits within.

COURTALL. Letters from whom?

PAGE. My lady sir; out of ye country.

COURTALL. Receive them and put them in the gilt cabinet. Her business is of no concernment. I have not leisure to peruse them now.   (*Exeunt.*

▼

Enter SIR WILLIAM MEANWELL; *his* LADY; MISTRESS FAITH, *her sister; and* RALPH.*

LADY MEANWELL. Sir are you ready to go with us? I admire   260
you trifle thus.*

MEANWELL. Dear mine, the coach is ready at the door. Do you and my sweet sister go before; and when I have dispatch'd with Ralph, I'll follow you.

LADY MEANWELL. You have not such affairs in the country but that you know no end of your discourse with Ralph. Your love to him is of a vast extent and reaches beyond all that a wife can merit from you— (*Weeps.*)

RALPH (*aside*). Plague a' those dissembling drops. May they poison the roses that they fall on to a leprosy.   270
(SIR WILLIAM *kisses his* LADY.)

MEANWELL. These drops flow from my heart which you profusely shed. I will leave all to go with thee.

LADY MEANWELL. By all that's good, you shall not. Those most afflict us whom we most do love. Each frivolous business snatches you from my enjoyment. Come, sister.

MEANWELL. Will you be pettish and not suffer me to go along with you now?

LADY MEANWELL. No, you shall first dispatch with your man, and come at his and your own pleasure.   (*Exeunt.*

MEANWELL. My wife has a many of strange crotchets in her   280

---

long a royal residence. This reference implies that Lord Courtall has connections with the very highest circles of society.

Enter . . . : the Meanwells' lodgings. Evening.

I admire you trifle thus: I am surprised that you delay.

head since she came to town. But change of soil may bring her to herself again.

RALPH. I have observed her much of late, and faith, sir, she is aware on't, which makes her haste you so to pack me into the country so soon. But if you keep her here long, it will undo you every way. I cannot fancy her night-revelling abroad, I know not where, whilst you at home lie dreaming of her coming still, but not of what she does. I admire you are not wonder'd at for a patient cuckold. 290

MEANWELL. I were worthy to be admir'd if I alone were such a horrible-headed beast as that thou speak'st of. But there are so many like me, if I be one, that the wonder can be nothing. But I dare swear my wife is very honest—

RALPH. That's the opinion of all wittols.*

MEANWELL. Wittol? What's that?

RALPH. Ninety-nine times a cuckold.*

MEANWELL. That's a many times indeed. My wife wept and sighed because I went not with her ere I dispatch'd with 300 thee. She is virtuous, though she has learn'd some cursed French freaks.

RALPH. My lady is witty. Would I were half as honest—

MEANWELL. Thou art malicious, and—

RALPH. Too much your honest servant.

MEANWELL. I cannot think my wife's a whore. I prithee hold thy tongue. I shall waste the time in vain, unnecessary chat with thee that should be us'd to send thee hence. Besides, I must not disappoint my friends. 'Tis time I were at the French lady's. 310

RALPH. I wish you'd please to let me wait upon you.

MEANWELL. Thy presence must distaste my wife. She hates thee.

RALPH. I will disguise me, sir, so that she shall not know me.

---

wittol: a contented cuckold, aware of and complacent about his wife's infidelity. Ralph may misunderstand the term, or his assertion that all wittols think their wives honest may be sarcastic.

ninety-nine times: we find no authority for this figure.

MEANWELL. About it, then, and as we go I will direct thee what to do when thou comest home. I'll fetch my sword,* and I am ready. (*Exeunt.*

▼

Enter SIR GREGORY, ZANY, RIGHTWIT, PHILARIO, *and* LEONORA.* [DRAWER *serves* SIR GREGORY, ZANY, *and* PHILARIO. LEONORA *talks to* RIGHTWIT *apart.*]

LEONORA. I wonder, brother, what your meaning is, to bring these witless puppies hither.

RIGHTWIT. You think this is handsome now. But faith, it 320
would become you better to smile than frown. Be wise, and use one of these "puppies" kindly, as you call them. They have that, that's much more precious nowadays than wit, beauty, or honesty: rich, plentiful estates. Although they are not favor'd with the noblest gifts of nature, their clothes and coin shall bear them out when wit and virtue—nay, and handsome faces too—are fast in cruel prisons lock'd and cannot show themselves but through a grate; which, when they do, who is't that looks at them? Take thy choice. One have I destin'd for thee. 330
Thou should'st have both by my consent, were it but lawful. You may use his estate you choose at your pleasure, and for variety what gallant you will. Nay, I durst be hang'd if him of the two thou accepts of will not kiss thy hand, and hold the door, he will be so indulgent.* What the plague would you be at?

LEONORA. I will see them both hang'd ere I will have either.

RIGHTWIT. Sir Gregory, Mr. Zany—put on. 'Slife, you'll never reach your journey's end else.*
[*To Drawer*] Some wine, you blockhead. A health to the 340
best proceeder.

(*Drink.*)

sword: worn by gentlemen in public as an article of formal dress.
Enter . . . : a tavern.
Nay, I durst . . . indulgent: Rightwit says that either fool will be so delighted to marry Leonora that he will countenance her horning him.
Sir Gregory . . . else: Rightwit urges them to drink so they can work up enough courage to propose to Leonora.

PHILARIO. And a horn for him that shall wed her.

RIGHTWIT. Peace, rascal.

ZANY. Madam, I declare you have my heart, and hope you'll use it well.

SIR GREGORY. You think to baffle me out of this bargain too, but I will see you hang'd first.

    [*To Leonora*] Mistress, I'll make you a lady. I am a person of honor, though my grandsire dealt in minerals.

    (*Aside*) That oaf would have told her if I had not.   350

    [*To Zany*] Give thy betters place.

RIGHTWIT. No quarrels, gentlemen. Your mistress' health.

ZANY. Let it go round— *

RIGHTWIT. Some music, boy, to grace it.

DRAWER. Here is not any in the house, sir.

RIGHTWIT. Nor nothing to make a noise with?

DRAWER. An old drum there is, within.

RIGHTWIT. Go tabor * on't, Philario.   [*Exit* PHILARIO.
    (*The drum within.*)

    Come gallants, let's drink this health—and the warlike drum shall echo the triumph of the pledge above the   360 highest element.

LEONORA. You care not how our credit suffers.

    (*Exit* LEONORA.

RIGHTWIT. Well, mistress, we shall follow ye anon.

ZANY. Ha? Where's the lady?

SIR GREGORY. A good jest. I' faith, she thinks to baffle us.

RIGHTWIT. She is nice and modest, as most virgins be. I'll bring you to her instantly.

SIR GREGORY. I love not to be baffled.

RIGHTWIT. Why ye shall not, sir. (*Sings.*)

        Give us more wine   370
        That's brisk and fine
        That we may drink
        Until we think
        That we are all divine.

Let it go round: Each member of the party reconfirms the toast.
tabor: to beat the tabor (a small drum).

SIR GREGORY (*sings*). Aye, more wine—
ZANY (*sings*). Till we are all divine.
PHILARIO. They are admirably drunk.
SIR GREGORY. Some music! There is an excellent new air—
every fiddler i'th' town can play it——oh, I could dance it
till I grew immortal.*   380
ZANY. So could I, but I never heard it in all my life. But, *non
abstante,** I'll do anything for company.
RIGHTWIT [*to Drawer*]. Go call some scrapers,* you rogue.
                                        [*Exit* DRAWER.
[*To Philario*] 'Twill make their physic work so well * that
we shall work them into anything.

Enter MUSICIANS.

RIGHTWIT. Come, my friends, play us a handsome reeling
antic. We are all ready, almost, to make indentures.*
Gallants, will you use your feet a little? They may grow
gouty else.
ZANY. We'll dance, and kick away such ill distemper from   390
them.
SIR GREGORY. A good motion, a good motion.
PHILARIO. Ah, that you should be hang'd for clipping our
good English so.* Strike up, you sons of Orpheus, and
charm our souls into activity, and make them, with your
lively strains, dance in us till we melt in pleasing rest,
and dream of new Elysiums.
(*They dance a reeling,** drunken antic * and go off the stage.

dance it till I grew immortal: Sir Gregory probably means he could dance it
forever.
  non abstante: Latin, "let us not be aloof."
  scrapers: a derogatory term for fiddlers.
  physic work so well: Dancing will make the wine take effect.
  indentures: (a) a contract—in this case to marry Leonora; (b) a zigzag
course—i.e., drink will make their dancing unsteady.
  hang'd for clipping our good English so: Philario's comment implies that
Sir Gregory and Zany speak with outlandish country accents. Only rarely,
however, is special pronunciation indicated by the spelling of their speeches.
  reeling: staggering. Evidently not "a reel," which is a lively dance with
couples facing each other and moving in figure eights.
  antic: a wild, grotesque dance.

▼

*The scene discover'd.** LORD COURTALL *and* MISTRESS FAITH, SIR FRANCIS MAKELOVE *and* LADY MEANWELL, *as plac'd severally, discoursing in the scene.*

FAITH. Your lordship much mistakes me. I do not look on every man.*

COURTALL. You are charitable then, for your eyes are utterly   400 destructive to all they dart their matchless glories on.

FAITH. Your lordship does romance with me, but by your language I perceive you are a rare historian.*

COURTALL (*aside*). She has charms above my frailty to resist. [*To Mistress Faith*] Madam, I am not so learn'd in the romance way as you conceive me, but yet I can discourse a story of my own, in your sweet ear, which, if you will with patience hear, shall in the close and sequel seem beyond what all the fluent'st poets feign in heathenish fiction. [COURTALL *whispers to* MISTRESS FAITH.]   410

LADY MEANWELL. 'Tis late: I shall be talk'd on. Sweet Makelove, my husband is no natural.*

Enter SIR WILLIAM MEANWELL, *and* RALPH *disguis'd.* [*They are not immediately noticed.*]

MEANWELL. How's this?

RALPH. Just as I told you.

MEANWELL. I hope not, yet I begin to suspect.

MAKELOVE. Madam, 'tis pity he should ever have enjoy'd such sweet perfection. I grieve to think on't—

LADY MEANWELL. I thought him tolerable till I saw you.

(*They kiss.*)

The scene . . . . Procreate's house during the evening.

look on every man: "to direct one's looks towards an object in contemplation" (*OED*). Faith is parrying a courtly love compliment with a naive—or perhaps disingenuous—assertion of her modesty. (For the manuscript reading, see the Textual Notes.)

historian: Faith may mean "storyteller," or she may just mean that Courtall's highflown compliments bespeak his acquaintance with chivalric romances.

natural: one deficient in intellect; a half-wit.

RALPH. Now, sir, what think you? Will you yet believe you are
a cuckold?   420

MEANWELL. Hold thy tongue, or I will make thee eat it.

LADY MEANWELL. Heaven and earth: my husband! Sir Francis, did I not say when first I saw Mr. Meanwell ap-
proach that I would use him * for disappointing us of his
company so long?
[*To Meanwell*] Nay, be angry and look scurvily. For 'tis
my aim to be reveng'd a little for the defeat you have
given us all this while in not letting us have you sooner.

MEANWELL. I do not like such odd revenges, madam. If 'tis
your pastime to afflict me, let your trim humour * prac-   430
tice some other way.   (*She weeps.*)

LADY MEANWELL. I never can be merry but you are horn-
mad.* I will go seek some wretched cave to languish out
my youth in where the sun's light, nor human conversation, ne'er shall find me.

RALPH [*aside*]. What excellent dissimulation's this?

MEANWELL (*aside to Ralph*). Dost thou see this, thou infidel?
How dar'st thou think I am a wittol, or a cuckold?
[*To his wife*] I do believe thou wast in jest, my dear. I
prithee don't afflict and shame me before all this com-   440
pany.

LADY MEANWELL. I am your shame.

Enter PROCREATE [*while* MEANWELL *apologizes*].

MEANWELL. I can scarce forbear to ask thee mercy for my
jealousy and rudeness before the whole congregation
here. But I will kneel to thee, my sweet, in private.
[*To Procreate*] Noblest lady, your pardon for my too long
absence. You eas'ly would forgive it if you knew how
much my soul, that better part, was with you.

PROCREATE. My roof is proud that you will deign to stoop beneath it. I will attend you instantly.   (*Exit.* 450

---

use him: to treat a person in a specified manner—in this case, harshly.
trim humour: capricious inclination.
horn-mad: insanely jealous; afraid of being cuckolded.

Music. The gallants compliment MEANWELL.* LORD COURT-
ALL *takes* MISTRESS FAITH *out to dance.*

MAKELOVE. Sir William, please to make your choice.

MEANWELL. I am not for these Court dances, which you of
the town are perfect in. Give me leave to look on and
learn.

MAKELOVE. Then, madam, since Sir William will stand out, I
do beseech you, let me have the honor to lead you. I can
but walk about.

LADY MEANWELL [*to Meanwell*]. Sweet mine, whom have you
with you?

MEANWELL. A friend, my dear, I met by chance. One that   460
you know not.

MAKELOVE. He shall please to make one— (*He brings a lady
to Ralph.*)

MEANWELL (*aside*). Ralph, thou wilt be out. Refuse it in
time.

RALPH. I'll try to do as they do, sir.

Enter PROCREATE.

PROCREATE. All pair'd in earnest? Sir William, we will not
stand for ciphers. You must not deny me.

MEANWELL. I know not, lady, what belongs to the new mode
of dancing. Let my ignorance excuse me.

PROCREATE. I'll teach you, then, as well as I can. Come, your   470
hand.

(*They all dance.*)

LADY MEANWELL [*to Meanwell*]. If I had been acquainted
with your skill in dancing, I should have been loath to
have seen you taken out by any other. But I perceive
there is none that is not more acceptable to you than me.
'Tis I that have most reason to be jealous—(*Seems to
weep.*)

compliment MEANWELL: Once the domestic squabble is ended, the other
men bow to Meanwell and formally acknowledge his presence at the party.

MEANWELL. Let me perish when I in thought deserve thy
jealousy. What I did was out of pure civility—

LADY MEANWELL. I know that tongue too well, but yet 't'as
power to charm me into anything. Be not disturb'd at my   480
too passionate love, for such is jealousy.

RALPH (*aside*). Ah, that thou art a cunning, plaguy witch,
and though thou palpably dost fool my master, I cannot
but love thy wit.

PROCREATE. Gallants, a slight banquet waits you within.

OMNES. We all wait upon you.   (*Exeunt.*

▼

Enter CLARABELL *and* MARK.*

CLARABELL. Oh, Mr. Mark! My father has rods in piss * for
you. Why, where have you been?

MARK. Guess, guess.

CLARABELL. In Hell, I think, thou look'st so like a fury.*   490

MARK. Troth, mistress, I was pretty near it, for I was dying
drunk, and certainly had I tripp'd afar with that distemper,* I had gone the plain pathway thither. But where's
my master?

CLARABELL. You'll know soon enough, to your cost, believe it.

MARK. Would there were no wine nor wenches in the world—

CLARABELL. 'Twould be well for you if there were not, for
then you might live sober and honest, perhaps—which
now I think you seldom do. But how do you think to
make your peace with my father? He's in a wicked pet *   500
against you.

MARK. Why, pretty mistress, will not you this once stand
'twixt me and danger?

Enter . . . : Swallow's office. The time is evening, two or three days later.
rods in piss: switches "curing" in vinegar, lye, or urine—with which he in-
tends to whip Mark; metaphorically, "punishment in store."
fury: an avenging or tormenting infernal spirit.
tripp'd afar with that distemper: The text appears corrupt here (see the
Textual Notes). The sense appears to be that had Mark gone far when that
drunk he would have wound up in Hell.
in a wicked pet: temper, especially a sulky fit of pique.

CLARABELL. I'll venture, conditionally you will leave your de-
baucheries and love your wife.

MARK. My wife, yes—and thousands besides. Do you think
me a heathen, to love no woman but my own? Faith, I
have more French religion * in me. (*He sings.*)

Song

He that one woman can satisfy
Is an enemy to his nation,   510
Since he with a score may multiply,
For its service, his generation.

Enter SWALLOW.

SWALLOW. Hey, I think the Devil has sent us a guest. Sirrha,
get you out. Here's no business for you.

MARK. Good sir, hear me.

SWALLOW. Well, sirrha: what is't you would say?

MARK. Anything to mitigate your worship's indignation
against me.
(*Aside to Clarabell*) Now, my witty she-devil, hast ne'er a
trick to fetch me off?   520

CLARABELL. You will not, sir, for his pure affection to you,
discard and turn him out of your service?

SWALLOW. How, affection to me? To be drunk two or three
days together?

CLARABELL. At first he was overcome with carousing too lib-
erally to your good health, I assure you.

SWALLOW. Pray, who told you so?

CLARABELL. My cousin Philario, one of the tribe—

SWALLOW. Of the drunkards. Where is that precious sot that
wanders up and down from one house of perdition to   530
another like one of the seed of Cain, to make fresh dis-
coveries of wine, pox, and wenches?

MARK. I left him sleeping upon an old broken bench.

French religion: love of sex.

SWALLOW. Would's neck were broken. Pray, sir, let your affection to me make you drunk no more. This once I
forgive your good nature. I must abroad to ferret out that
bankrupt, Rightwit. I'll lay him fast enough * before I
sleep. Look to my gates.   (*Exit.*

CLARABELL [*aside*]. Ha? What have I heard this wicked old
man talk of? Nothing but ruining the man I love more 540
than the world does light. The kindness that my heart
has for poor Rightwit must not suffer his undoing thus.
[*To Mark*] Mark? I have a frolic. Prithee fetch me a suit,
out of Philario's chamber, of his apparel. I'll turn boy for
an hour or two. Away, and bring me with it all things
necessary.

MARK. You may serve for a girl in boy's habit.* The trick is
common.

CLARABELL. Leave your prophecies and be naught * awhile,
and do what I command you. So slow? I'll do't myself— 550

MARK. I go, mistress, I go. But what is't you design?

CLARABELL. You shall not know.

                          (MARK *offers to go.*)
Stay—I had forgot to ask you where you left Philario.

MARK. At the Half Moon Tavern,* in the Strand.   [*Exit.*

CLARABELL. Rightwit and he are inseparable. They are soul
and body.

---

lay him fast enough: literally, put him in fetters or imprison him. Collo-
quially, the expression has somewhat the force of "settle his hash." Cf. Otway's *Cheats of Scapin,* I,i: "I know how to lay that rogue my son fast."
Swallow proposes to have Rightwit arrested for debt.

You may serve . . . boy's habit: Mark may be saying that Clarabell will be
able to "pass" as a boy. Judging from her response, however, he means that
she will look like a girl despite her disguise. Use of this device was popular
throughout the period; it allowed actresses to show off their legs in tight
pants. Such "breeches roles" were used extensively in Dryden's *Rival Ladies*
(1664), Betterton's popular *The Woman Made a Justice* (1670), and many
other plays.

be naught: keep quiet (imperative).

Half Moon Tavern: A tavern with this name was visited by Pepys, 10 June
1663. Several taverns had the same name: probably the one near Bedford
Street on the Strand is meant. For other possibilities see J. Paul de Castro, "A
Dictionary of the Principal London Taverns since the Restoration," 4 vols.
(ca. 1927), Guildhall MS. 3110.

If Love guide me right,
I will to Rightwit show my love this night.

(*Exit.*

▼

Enter LORD COURTALL *and* PROCREATE.*

COURTALL. They are all coach'd. I think 'tis pretty late. (*Looks on a watch.*)
PROCREATE. What hour is't, my lord?   560
COURTALL. But early, yet not ten. I thought it had been more. Madam, three words and I am gone.
PROCREATE. Say on, my lord.
COURTALL. My life is in your hands. Let me in whisper tell you what my soul would speak. (*He whispers.*)
PROCREATE. How! Your lordship in love with Madam Faith, my Lady Meanwell's sister? Though 'tis possible she (being young and innocent) may be seduc'd—I do protest I will not for a world—
COURTALL. Hold, madam. Forswear nothing but leaping over 570 steeples backward. I'll marry you to a young, rich country knight. You are a widow, and in a strange nation. 'Tis good to have a settlement. Will you oblige me or not? If you are of that soft and thawing temper you imply— Methinks you should not let me, for her, die.
PROCREATE. A young, rich, country knight? Well, my lord, you have such an influence over my soul that it has not a motion * but shall work for you. But things must be carried cunningly. Yet—
COURTALL. What "yet"? Why do you demur thus?   580
PROCREATE. Your lordship will make good your word to me?
COURTALL. Upon my soul and honor.
PROCREATE. The offence to Heaven is great in doing such a sin—

Enter . . . : Procreate's house at the end of another party. The time is almost 10 P.M.
motion: an inward prompting or impulse.

COURTALL. Scruples of conscience? Fie, madam, they suit
　　not with your, nor my, designs.
　　　　Please to withdraw, and let's consult within,
　　　　How I th' enjoyment of my love may win.

　　　　　　　　　　　　　　　　　　　　　(Exeunt.

　　　　　　[End of Act II]

ACT THE THIRD

RIGHTWIT, PHILARIO, SIR GREGORY, MR. ZANY, *as in a tavern.**

RIGHTWIT. More wine, you rogue, and lights, for these grow
dim. Give us some fresh, and glasses to the brim—

Enter DRAWER *with wine and lights.*

DRAWER. A pretty young gentleman desires to speak with Mr.
Rightwit.
RIGHTWIT. Villain, slave, did I not say at my entrance that I
would speak with no one?

Enter CLARABELL.

CLARABELL. Oh, sir, you must.
RIGHTWIT. How? "Must," bastard?
CLARABELL. Yes, must, sir. Or 'tis no matter, there is some-
what will speak to you. You might have given the bearer   10
gentler language. (*Gives him a paper.*)
[*Aside*] There's witchcraft in his—looks and I must—fly
it—   (*Exit* CLARABELL.
RIGHTWIT. Philario, a word—
PHILARIO. If thou wilt hence with me, well and good. That
rogue "boy" is a trepan * and I must follow him. If not,
I'll after him alone.
RIGHTWIT. Wilt thou hear me—

tavern: The time is later the same night.
trepan: a cheating rogue. Specifically, one who decoys a person into a position which may work to his loss or ruin.

96

PHILARIO. 'Sdeath, 'a will be gone—   (*Exit.*

RIGHTWIT. The fellow's mad. This pretty boy has brought a   20
ticket * from some friend—I know not whom—which
tells me that Swallow is watching here i'th' street for me.
If this unknown friend should be his pretty, roguish
daughter, now—I'll follow Philario and see the event of
. his madness and inform myself without, if the lad be not
. yet got out o'th' house.
[*To Sir Gregory and Zany*] Gentles, will you please to
laugh away six minutes till I return?
                                        (*He draws a pistol.*)
(*Aside*) Swallow and his setting dogs shall have hot service if they begin their work.   (*Exit.*   30

ZANY. Faith, I see nothing to laugh at.

SIR GREGORY. Pish, man, we'll laugh at one another.

ZANY. Aye, so we may. For I suspect this wicked hector * has
left us in the lash * for the reckoning. His fellow beagle
slunk first away, and now he's follow'd.

SIR GREGORY. They shall be hang'd ere they shall baffle us.
Let's withdraw and try if we can scent 'em.   (*Exeunt.*

▼

Enter CLARABELL *pursued by* PHILARIO.*

PHILARIO. How now, have I catch'd you? You are very
nimble. Confess, you rogue, which way you purchas'd
your trappings that you have on. Are you studying for an   40

ticket: note, billet.
hector: a swaggering ruffian, a tough.
in the lash: in the lurch.
Enter . . . : another part of the tavern. The location cannot be the street,
since Swallow's minions are waiting there to arrest Rightwit. The simplest
way to stage the pursuit would be to let the reappearance of Clarabell and
Philario through a proscenium door indicate that the forestage is now a sepa-
rate place, and not change the set. However, in line 72.1, Polwhele specifies
that the tavern is "discovered again." She may have forgotten about Swallow's ambush for the moment. A Restoration company might have coped
with the problem by dropping the curtain briefly. For a discussion of such
use of the curtain cá. 1670, see Montague Summers, *The Restoration Theatre* (1934; rpt. New York: Humanities Press, 1964), pp. 158–165.

invention? * I'll bring you to those which shall examine you, ye young picaroon.* Come along.

Enter RIGHTWIT.

RIGHTWIT. How now, Philario? Why dost thou abuse the youth?

CLARABELL. Loose me, ye son of mischief!

PHILARIO. Clarabell!

RIGHTWIT. How, Clarabell? Sweet, charitable soul. Thou art so prettily metamorphos'd that, hang me if I knew thee. Let me hug thee.

CLARABELL. Away. You shall not conjure me within the circle   50
of your arms.

RIGHTWIT. Why so shy? I know thou lov'st me.

CLARABELL. For which of your ill conditions, think you?

RIGHTWIT. For my good ones altogether.

CLARABELL. I wish I knew you had any. I could the better justify my passion. Well, keep yourself sober enough to fear the danger I have told you of. [*She offers to leave.*]

RIGHTWIT. Nay, my dear she-rogue. Come with us to the tavern and droll away one little hour. There's none will know thee. And yet, in faith, Zany and *Stultus* * were   60
with us. And there, I do believe, they stay our coming.

CLARABELL. 'Tis very late, and yet I have a mind to go and put some trick upon the widgeons * to make us merry. They are such fools they'll never know me. But stay. What time of night is't?

PHILARIO. Scarce the eleventh hour. But what if the old ruffian should go * home, and miss "his only Clarabell"?

CLARABELL. Let Mark alone to make my apology: "Clarabell's gone not well to bed."

---

studying for an invention: thinking up a (false) story.
picaroon: rogue, knave, scoundrel.
Stultus: Latin for "fool."
widgeons: wild ducks, regarded as especially stupid birds.
should go: added by the editors.

RIGHTWIT. Why, thou may'st stay till day. Let's to the tavern.   70
  March—
PHILARIO. Away, away.   (*Exeunt.*

▼

The tavern discover'd again, with SIR GREGORY, MR. ZANY, *and* DRAWER.

SIR GREGORY. I never will be baffled so again.
ZANY. Ne'er stir,* if henceforth I do not shut my eyes with as
  great indignation at the sight of a tavern, as at home I do
  my gates against the beggars.
SIR GREGORY [*to Drawer*]. Well, here's one half of thy reckoning, fellow, since it must be so.
ZANY. And here's the other. Thou might'st be so good-natur'd
  as to give us some back.   80
DRAWER. Your worship is merry!

Enter RIGHTWIT, PHILARIO, CLARABELL.

ZANY. See, Sir Gregory. As I live, they are return'd again.
SIR GREGORY. Pox on't. What luck had we to pay the reckon-
  ing! I'll be hang'd if they do not baffle us.
RIGHTWIT. Gentlemen, your pardons. Here is a pretty youth
  detain'd me about some business beyond the time I
  promis'd to return.
SIR GREGORY (*aside*). I would the "pretty youth" were hang'd
  for's labor.
CLARABELL. How dull this place is. No wine or ladies?   90
  [*To Drawer*] Sirrha, have you no women in the house?
DRAWER. Not of note, but my mistress.
SIR GREGORY [*to Zany*]. What little he-devil's this?

Ne'er stir: a mild expletive, perhaps equivalent to "by gosh." Harold F.
Brooks has suggested to us that the phrase was a Puritan asseveration or
substitute for profanity, citing Brome's line: "Gods nigs and ne'er stir, sir,
has vanquished God damn me." The phrase is used six times in *The Country
Gentleman* (1669).

ZANY. A young cock-chicken of the game,* you may perceive
by him. Let us comply with them, to get our money
again—or part of it.

SIR GREGORY. Agreed.

CLARABELL [to Drawer]. Entreat thy mistress to come hither.
And—dost thou hear?—get us a noise of scrapers.*
There's for thy pains. [Gives him money.]   100

DRAWER. I'll do't instantly.   (Exit DRAWER.

RIGHTWIT. I am a rogue if I do not love thee better and better.
Thou and I should beget an excellent race of merry bastards. When shall's * try?

CLARABELL. Never. I will hatch all I breed in England. I hear
they are sending you to one of the uninhabited islands.
You are wotted * to be so good at the act of generation
that 'tis thought in a short time you would go near to
people a New World.

RIGHTWIT. With a little of thy help. I have much ado to for-   110
bear kissing thee—

(She laughs at him and sings.)

Song

Thou shalt not touch my lips,
Nor anything else that is warm.
I know thou wilt do me no good,
And, by God, thou shalt do me no harm.

RIGHTWIT. The rogue is full of humour.

CLARABELL. Why droop you, gallants? No wine, nor music? I
shall grow sluggish too. Oh, here comes that will wake
us.

cock-chicken of the game: i.e., "he" is a cocky young womanizer. "The
game" has amorous connotations, though its basic meaning is "pastime."
The referent of "him" at the end of the sentence is not made clear.

get us a noise of scrapers: get us some music—a swaggering and somewhat contemptuous demand. Clarabell is playing rakehell with spirit. The
anonymous author of The Woman turn'd Bully (1675) develops such a situation at length.

shall's: shall us, an obsolete seventeenth-century form of the first person
plural present of shall.

wotted: known (past participle of wot). The first OED citation of this form
is to Scott's Rob Roy (1818).

Enter DRAWER *with his* MISTRESS *and* FIDDLERS. CLARABELL
*kisses her and then begins her health.**

ZANY. This is the smartest * rascal.   120
SIR GREGORY. Let him be as smart as 'a will, he shall be
  hang'd ere he shall baffle us. Here's a health to the gentlewoman. (*Drinks.*)
CLARABELL. I'll see't go round.

Enter MARK, *disguis'd.*

MARK. A word, young gentleman, with you.
CLARABELL. Mark! What the Devil brings thee hither?
MARK. The night being far spent, my master so weary grew of
  watching for your Rightwit, that he came home and 's
  gone to bed, sending me in his room.* My ministers are
  ready o'er the way to snap him when 'a does come out.* 130
CLARABELL. They shall be hang'd first. Rightwit, a word.
                                          (*They whisper.*)
RIGHTWIT. Fortune grows kind and civil to me after her
  scurvy usage.
CLARABELL. I have a project in my pate—let me pursue it.
  [*To the fiddlers*] Strike up, you rascals. Play me the new
  air call'd "The Frolics."
                                  (*They play it once over.*)
CLARABELL. You are perfect in it. 'Tis an admirable, stirring
  dance. But we want women. Let some of us disguise and
  act them.
RIGHTWIT. 'Twould be a handsome frolic and worth talking 140
  on.
SIR GREGORY. 'Tis *à la mode* to be talk'd on. I will be one that
  will disguise. I'll not be baffled.
ZANY. I have personated Maid Marian in a country morris *

  begins her health: starts the ritual by which the toast is passed all around
the company.
  smartest: literally, quick, active, prompt. By connotation, sharp and cocky.
  in his room: in his place.
  snap . . . out: The bailiffs will arrest Rightwit when he comes out on the
public street.
  country morris: On morris dancing see I, 109, above. The part of Maid
Marian was often danced by a boy.

when I was a boy, and have been held to do it well. Pray let me act the other. I am sure I can perform 't.

CLARABELL. No question. Mistress, can you do us the favor to furnish us with some clothes?

MISTRESS. Yes, sir. If they will please to walk along with me.

ZANY. Halloo, halloo, let's go!   (*Exeunt.*   150

RIGHTWIT. Honest Mark, a brimmer— (*Drinks.*)

CLARABELL. Hold, thou wilt make him drunk.

PHILARIO. Clarabell, thou wert always a good wench, but I never lov'd thee heartily till now.

CLARABELL. Very well—oh, here come the ladies.*

[*Enter* SIR GREGORY *and* MR. ZANY, *disguised, with the* MISTRESS *of the tavern.*]

How they strive which shall woman it best! 'Tis rare sport. I would not have miss'd it for an empire.

RIGHTWIT. We are beholden to thee for it. I may chance requite thee with better.

CLARABELL. Were ever such a pair of ugly manikins seen?   160

RIGHTWIT. Well, here I make my choice. (RIGHTWIT *takes the* MISTRESS.)

CLARABELL. Hah. There is but one woman, and you must snap her.

RIGHTWIT. Art jealous?

CLARABELL. No, faith. Drawer, make us out with my man. He should have disguis'd too, but 'tis late. Come fiddlers, "The Frolics."

(*They dance. The dance being ended,* RIGHTWIT *and* PHILARIO *dance off. Then* CLARABELL *takes* SIR GREGORY *out and dances a jig.*)

---

here come . . . ladies: The author has allowed far too little time offstage for the change of clothes. To stage this scene a director would have to interpolate another song or dance at this point, or to place the change of costume in sight on stage during the following conversation. If the latter were done, the fools' clothes would have to be taken away by a servant, since Zany and Gregory subsequently go off stage in search of them.

CLARABELL. Ha? Where are my comrades that brought me
in? All vanish'd? This 'tis to keep company with sharks,*
fellows that have no more money than religion. 'Tis   170
likely they have left me in the lash for the reckoning.

ZANY [aside]. Sir Gregory, this villainous young snap will
leave us in the lurch except we outwit him. He has a
damnable cunning, rascally look. Under color of disrob-
ing ourselves, let us go out with a promise to return, and,
when we have got our own clothes on our backs, outslip
him, and cozen * him that would cozen us.

SIR GREGORY. 'Twill be rare. We'll do't and laugh at him
hereafter wherever we meet him, ha, ha, ha.

ZANY. 'Tis witty, ha! Is't not witty?   180

SIR GREGORY. I could hug thee for the conceit. Ha, ha, ha.

CLARABELL. You are monstrous merry, sirs.

ZANY. We will go and unvest * and wait of you again.
[Aside] This will do me more good than if I had recover'd
our reckoning money.   (Exeunt.

CLARABELL. Drawer?

DRAWER. Ready, sir.

CLARABELL. What is the reckoning?

DRAWER. Two pieces.* Besides, the music is unpaid.

CLARABELL. Reckon it five—and keep these coxcombs safe   190
till thou art paid. There's for thee. [Gives him money.]

DRAWER. If they flinch,* hang me.

CLARABELL. Away, Mark.

(Exeunt severally, CLARABELL with MARK, FIDDLERS with
DRAWER and MISTRESS.

Enter ZANY and SIR GREGORY, as making unready.*

sharks: A shark is "a worthless and impecunious person who gains a pre-
carious living by sponging on others, . . . a parasite" (OED).

cozen: to cheat or defraud, particularly under pretense of friendship or
"cousinship."

unvest: remove their female garb. Used as a reflexive and absolute verb
this way, the term is usually applied to ecclesiastical vestments.

Two pieces: slang for guinea gold coins. This is an enormous bill; Clarabell, the audience must gather, is decidedly well-to-do.

flinch: sneak off (now an obsolete meaning).

as making unready: undressed, or in the process of undressing.

SIR GREGORY. These rogues have left their lousy skins for us
to wear, instead of our own good vestments! The cheat
was a-acting whilst we danc'd that wicked jig.
ZANY. No harm, Sir Gregory. That politic tyke, Rightwit, fears
arresting. We may have our clothes again. 'Twas but his
frolic to escape the bailies.*
SIR GREGORY. If it be nothing else,   200

    Let's put on those he and his comrogue *
      have left * and away,
    And leave the rascal that's within to pay.

                              (*Exeunt.*

[End of Act III]

bailies: bailiffs, warrant officers who execute writs and processes, distrains,
and arrests. Swallow has a warrant out for Rightwit's arrest for debt.
comrogue: fellow-rogue, comrade. A slang term popular ca. 1670.
Let's put on . . . left: The author does not make clear why the fools
resume their female garb instead of taking the clothes left by Rightwit and
Philario. Possibly they are interrupted before they can make the change. In
the next scene (as we later realize) Rightwit directs a constable to arrest the
hapless pair.

ACT THE FOURTH

RIGHTWIT *and* PHILARIO *pursued by* SPEAK *and* PLAINMAN.*

PLAINMAN. God's nownes, you hacksters,* we will make sure
on you. Oh, my master, my master, that ever I should
see "another rogue in thy skin," * as the saying is. O constable? Where's the constable?

SPEAK. A pox upon you, where are you, constable?

Enter CONSTABLE.

CONSTABLE. Keep the peace here. What's the matter, Mr.
Rightwit?

RIGHTWIT. I know no more than you, but two counterfeit
country rogues * have set upon us here and, I imagine,
would have stripp'd us, had we not call'd you.   10

SPEAK. Oh, lie! 'Twas we that call'd the constable.

RIGHTWIT. I pray you send them to the roundhouse * instantly.

CONSTABLE. I will.

RIGHTWIT. I have some other business for you too. A word—
(*Whispers.*)

RIGHTWIT . . . : the street, later that night.
hacksters: ruffians; prostitutes' bullies.
"another rogue in thy skin": spoken as a proverb, though we have not
identified it. "Skin" is occasionally used figuratively for "clothes" in this
period.
counterfeit country rogues: thieves or footpads pretending to be simple
countrymen.
roundhouse: a lock-up; a temporary place of detention for arrested persons.

PLAINMAN. Roundhouse? God's nownes, where's that?

CONSTABLE. Come along. Ye shall know soon enough. Good
    morrow, sir.   (*Exeunt severally.*

▼

Enter SIR WILLIAM MEANWELL *in his nightgown, and*
RALPH.*

MEANWELL. 'Tis very early. I think I must to bed again.
    Ralph, will you homewards today?   20

RALPH. I had rather stay, sir, till I can perceive you a little
    more inclin'd to follow me. A word in your ear, if ye
    please sir. (*Whispers.*)

MEANWELL. I prithee get thee gone. There will be no end of
    my horns if thou stay'st a little longer.
                                    (*Exit* MEANWELL.

RALPH. Thou art a fool, a cuckoldly fool, and I will make thee
    see thy horns, though they hang in thy light and over-
    shadow all natural sense and reason.   (*Exit.*

▼

Enter JUSTICE SWALLOW, CLARABELL, MARK, *and the* CON-
STABLE *with* SIR GREGORY *and* ZANY *in their women's habits.**

SWALLOW. How now: what are these?

CONSTABLE. Ladies of pleasure, and't please your worship. An   30
    honest gentleman, a neighbor of mine, charg'd me to
    apprehend them at a tavern and bring them before your
    worship.

CLARABELL [*aside*]. Oh, how I love this Rightwit and his
    wicked wit! He has gone beyond me in this frolic,
    clearly. I meant them no more mischief than the reckon-
    ing came to.

SWALLOW. Ladies of pleasure, dost thou call them? There is
    but little pleasure in them, sure.

Enter . . . : the Meanwells' lodging.
Enter . . . : Swallow's office, early the next morning.

CLARABELL. I am of opinion that they carried love letters be-   40
    twixt Dido and Aeneas,* they are such strange, old,
    moded gentlewomen.
CONSTABLE. Your worship being a just man, and a lover of
    the Cause,* I hope will punish for example these lewd
    beasts in petticoats, not worthy to be styl'd "women."
SWALLOW. I profess their very looks give me two stomachs,
    one to vomit, another to purge. Prithee take them
    hence and whip them into honesty.
MARK [aside]. Rare sport, mistress!
CLARABELL [aside]. No, here is not company enough to laugh   50
    at it, so the jest is spoil'd.
ZANY. Whipp'd? I never could endure that, of a little child.*
    Worshipful Justice Swallow, will you not know your old
    friend Isaac Zany?
CLARABELL (aside). Yes, to be as very an ass as e'er he was.
SWALLOW. How? Mr. Zany!
ZANY. The very same.
SIR GREGORY. I'll not be baffled with the whip. Sir, to beget
    your wonder bigger with child, behold your friend and
    servant Gregory, who in time may become your son-in-   60
    law.
CLARABELL [aside]. Thou shalt become the gallows first.
SWALLOW. Constable, I discharge thee, and will answer for
    these gentlemen.   (Exit CONSTABLE.
    I do perceive you have, by some bad company, been
    much misled. Within, I pray you let me understand upon
    what score you have thrown by your sex and unadvisedly
    thus put on another. Your men for some miscarriage
    were committed to the roundhouse, from whence (out of
    my respect to you) I have releas'd them, they sending   70
    hither with a belief you had been here. I pray you both,

---

    betwixt Dido and Aeneas: Virgil, *Aeneid*, I and IV. Clarabell is saying, with
sarcastic gentility, that as whores they are decidedly long in the tooth, and ri-
diculously unattractive.
    the Cause: puritanism; hence the Constable's recommendation of a harsh
sentence for the two "whores."
    of a little child: even when I was a child.

withdraw with me. Clarabell, I'll see you shall have a husband that shall like ye.

CLARABELL (*aside*). You shall be blind, else.   (*Exeunt.*

▼

LORD COURTALL *and* MISTRESS FAITH *discovered, he kissing and hugging her hand.**

COURTALL. How fair, and soft, and sweet, and melting 'tis. Who would not with his life's purchase buy the riches of your love? None but a eunuch.

FAITH. A eunuch? What's that, my lord?

COURTALL. A creature, the most insensible of all creatures. Nay, you'll not deny a modest kiss? In lieu of which, receive this diamond.   80

To them, PROCREATE.

PROCREATE. *Très homble serviteur.* You both must think my absence very rude, but I have added to my house a drawing room which three days since was finish'd; and now my business has been, all this morn, to furnish it. The pictures are all plac'd, the looking glasses hung, the carpets spread, and everything in order set. Nothing is wanting, but your noble presence. I design to treat you there. The maidenhead of the place cannot resign itself to nobler guests.   90

(*Aside*) My lord, how go affairs?

COURTALL. Pretty handsomely.

PROCREATE. I will presume to lead the way.   (*Exeunt.*

▼

Enter MAKELOVE *and* LADY MEANWELL.*

MAKELOVE. But is 'a jealous, madam?

LADY MEANWELL. Almost to lunacy. You must feign a pre-

LORD COURTALL . . . . : Procreate's house, time around midday.
Enter . . . . : The setting is probably the Meanwells' quarters.

tense to my sister: she is young and single and has a fortune.* We must persuade Mr. Meanwell you address to
her, or we must correspond no more.

MAKELOVE. I'll order things so handsomely that he shall
swear't. But here 'a comes.   100

[*Enter* MEANWELL.]

LADY MEANWELL. Pray leave us. Let me alone with him.
                              (*Exit* MAKELOVE.
Dearest Meanwell, why so melancholy?

MEANWELL. You shall be satisfied. It is my grief and shame
that he who left you now has robb'd me of your heart
and conversation, so that my own slaves* grow im-
pudent enough upon't to call me cuckold.

LADY MEANWELL. Heaven and earth, cannot I be familiar
with a gallant but I must be wicked? I am intimate with
no person except your too-much-loved self and him—but
only intimate with him for to prefer my sister. He knows 110
no end of his estate; and all I aim at is only to contract a
match betwixt them—if you ruin not my design with idle
jealousy, and gambolling down into the country, ere I
have perfected the work I have begun.

MEANWELL. By Heaven and Hell! I never will suspect thee
more. I'll wink at your familiarity and countenance everything you act in that concern. Forgive and pardon,
Sweet, my causeless, wicked jealousy this once, I
prithee. I will offend no more.

LADY MEANWELL. Look you do not.   120

MEANWELL. So you will seal my pardon. (*He kisses her.*)
(*Aside*) I will cut this rogue's throat—my man. But yet
he knew not my wife's plot. He is a fool. But I dare swear
I am no cuckold. I will go tell him all.
[*To Lady Meanwell*] Come, dear mine.   (*Exeunt.*

has a fortune: This is untrue. Faith is trying to "pass for a fortune," aided
by her sister. We learn in a later scene that Makelove has been told she is
without money, but after Lord Courtall persuades him otherwise, he jumps
at the chance to marry her.
slaves: servants.

▼

Enter RIGHTWIT *pursued by two or three* WOMEN.*

RIGHTWIT. Ye she-goats, you will not ravish me?
WOMEN. Have we catch't you? You are not to be found of late
by your friends. Pull him in, and hear him not. 'A has a
tongue would tempt the Devil, were he a woman.*
*(They pull him in.**)

Enter PHILARIO.

PHILARIO. Where the Devil should this Rightwit be? I have   130
wander'd from one good old haunt to another to find
him, but in vain. He is absolutely lost. These ruins use to
be propitious to our encounters, and here we often stum-
ble on one another——ha?

Enter RIGHTWIT, *bound, with two children tied upon his
back.*

RIGHTWIT. So, this I pay for smock service.* 'Twould never
grieve me, if I were sure the burden I carry were my
own. But who knows rightly who's the father of a
whore's child?
(They cry.)
This is worse than all the rest. The Lord take you to his
mercy.   140
PHILARIO. Rightwit?
RIGHTWIT. Philario! Good lad, undo me.

Enter CLARABELL.

Enter . . . : The setting is a street, near some "ruins" at a distance from
Swallow's house. The time is midday.
were he a woman: This conceit testifies to Rightwit's sex appeal.
They pull him in: into what is not specified—perhaps an alley. This is in
effect an exit; the women do not reappear on stage.
smock service: A smock is a female undergarment—a slip or shift. Smock
service means service by a woman with connotations "suggestive of immo-
rality," as the *OED* observes. Examples of "smock" compounds are numerous in seventeenth-century drama. Cf. the modern slang "servicing a
man," or the agricultural term "stud service."

CLARABELL. That were pity, in faith: you are so well done.*

RIGHTWIT. What Devil sent thee so far from home to disturb
　　our business?

CLARABELL. Thou look'st just like the monster * with three
　　heads, one growing out of each shoulder and the third
　　where it should, i'th' middle.

RIGHTWIT. Hold thy prating and untie me.

CLARABELL. Lord, that you should be so weary of what, no   150
　　doubt, you purchas'd willingly.

PHILARIO. Peace. Here's company not far off.

CLARABELL. The knight and Zany! Fortune could not provide
　　thee two such asses again to bear thy luggage for thee.
　　I'll help thee, if thou wilt swear to clap it on their shoul-
　　ders.

RIGHTWIT. By my vexation, I will.

CLARABELL. I must hide me. Quick, quick—why so slow, Don
　　Quixote? * (She unbinds him and skips aside.)

RIGHTWIT. Away, Philario, to the old place and bespeak a dish   160
　　for dinner. I can do this alone.　　　　　　(Exit PHILARIO.

Enter SIR GREGORY and MR. ZANY.

SIR GREGORY. See, Mr. Zany, as I breathe; Rightwit and two
　　on's bastards, as sure as can be. The heathenish rogue
　　will go near to hang them upon our backs.

ZANY. By this light that shines, will he if he can. I dare not
　　run for fear he should follow and beat me. It is a wicked,
　　hectorian rascal. We must use our wits. The while I
　　greet him, slip you behind him and clap this girdle
　　about's arms, and we'll bind him. 'Twill be a rare re-
　　venge for all his tricks.　　　　　　　　　　　　　　170

　　done: slang for hoaxed, overreached.
　　monster: Freaks and "monsters" of various sorts (dwarfs, giants, her-
maphrodites, siamese twins, deformed fetuses) were exhibited at fairs and in
street booths. We cannot identify this particular monster. Henry Morley, in
Memoirs of Bartholomew Fair, rev. ed. (London: Chatto and Windus, 1880),
pp. 245–258, records some two-headed freaks on display, but none with
three.
　　Don Quixote: The meaning of this joking identification is not very clear.
Clarabell is evidently mocking Rightwit by likening him to that determined
but ineffectual performer of "heroic" deeds.

SIR GREGORY. And we will bind his bastards on his back, and serve him as, a thousand to one, he would serve us.

RIGHTWIT. You are serious, gallants.

SIR GREGORY. We came to wait of our mistress to a house-rearing; * but harkening to some very rare ballad singers, we lost her, unluckily, amongst the crowd. There is no wit like that in ballads.*

RIGHTWIT. 'Tis not amiss that she is out o'th' way. I have some certain tokens to deliver to you both from noble gentlewomen of your acquaintance that might have dis- 180 humor'd her.

SIR GREGORY. Oh, have you so, sir?

(*They bind him.* CLARABELL *peeps and laughs.*)

RIGHTWIT. How now? Rascals, cowards, slaves! I'll eat you! Loose me, or by—

ZANY. No swearing now, sir. 'Twill do no good.

SIR GREGORY. Pray, sir, look well to your carriages * here.

(*They tie the children again on's back.* CLARABELL *stands as unseen, laughing.*)

ZANY. Pray commend us to the gentlewomen ye spoke of. And see the children have cleanly pap and dry clouts.* They may be pissburnt, else. Ha, ha, ha!

SIR GREGORY. Fare you well, sir, and be sure you are not 190 deficient in your care of them. Ha, ha, ha! (*Exit ambo.**)

Enter CLARABELL.

CLARABELL. The gentlemen advis'd you well. I hope you'll take their counsel, for the good of your little ones.

RIGHTWIT. Plague on them, and thee too! Unbind me once more, or get out of my sight.

house-rearing: not in the *OED*. Presumably a house-warming ceremony is meant. Less plausibly, something analogous to the American "house-raising" could be intended.

no wit . . . ballads: an obviously fatuous statement betraying Sir Gregory's simplicity.

your carriages: what you are carrying.

cleanly pap and dry clouts: wholesome milk and dry diapers.

Exit ambo: Latin for "both exit."

CLARABELL. If I unbind thee, hang me. Nay, you may look like an ass well enough, to let Sir Gregory and Zany coax * you thus, the veriest gulls in nature. Ha, ha, ha!

RIGHTWIT. Imp of Lucifer.

CLARABELL. Frothy-brain'd Rightwit.   200

RIGHTWIT. I will never see thy face again.

CLARABELL. Why, what? Thou dost not mean to hang thyself?

RIGHTWIT. Get hence.

CLARABELL. Not till I have tir'd myself with laughing.

RIGHTWIT. I will not throw away another word upon thee.

CLARABELL. Yes, yes. If it be nothing but railing, it cannot vex me.

RIGHTWIT. No, that's the plague on't. Therefore I will be silent.   210

CLARABELL. Nay, if you turn mummer, I am gone.   (*Exit.*

RIGHTWIT. The pox go with thee!

Enter PHILARIO.

PHILARIO. What, loaded still? No wonder that you stay'd so long. Where's Clarabell? How chance the rascal holpe * you not?

RIGHTWIT. Ask me no wounding questions, but help me.
                                          (PHILARIO *unbinds him.*)

PHILARIO. Down with thy burden, quick. My uncle, I see my uncle. Clap on this beard.* He bends his course this way.

RIGHTWIT. 'Tis he? I'll meet the rascal with my own face.   220

PHILARIO. Thou art not mad?

RIGHTWIT [*to children*]. Come up here. I'll provide you a foster father.   (*Exit with children.*

PHILARIO. I'll follow at a distance and see the event of this.
                                                                  (*Exit.*

coax: make a "cokes" of, befool, impose on.
holpe: obsolete past tense of "to help."
beard: Polwhele uses this convention seriously in Act V of *The Faithful Virgins,* where no one recognizes a would-be rapist as the Duke of Tuscany until Cleophon "pulls off his false beard."

▼

Soft music and a song within. The scene opens,* LORD
COURTALL *and* MISTRESS FAITH *in it.*

COURTALL. Let me breathe away my soul in kisses on these
lips—
FAITH. You have kiss'd too much already. I fear you have un-
done me, my lord.
COURTALL. Fear nothing. It comes with a fear.*
            (*He leads her out of the scene. Scene closes.**

▼

Enter MARK *and* CLARABELL.*

CLARABELL. Nay, sweet Mark, run and release him from his   230
ill-favor'd burden. But I charge thee, do not say I sent
thee. We are fallen out.
MARK. Ha? Mistress—
CLARABELL. Look here, Mark. What's this? My father?
MARK. 'Tis very like him.

Enter SWALLOW *bound, with the children on's back.*

CLARABELL [*aside*]. This infidel Rightwit hath done this to
abuse him! 'Twas a heathenish trick; yet I must dote on
him for it. But hang him, sure he loves me not, or he'd
have found some other beast to have borne his rubbish
for him than my father.   240
[*To Swallow*] Lord, sir, what have you brought us here?
[*Aside*] I can't forbear laughing, for my heart.
SWALLOW. Audacious hilding,* I'll make you wear a face less

---

scene opens . . . : The new room in Procreate's house is revealed.
   Fear . . . fear: The text is evidently corrupt here. The author seems to
have dropped a line (or more) in the process of copying.
   He leads . . . Scene closes: The point of this stage direction is hard to see,
since if the shutters close there is no need for an exit as such.
   Enter . . . : the street, early afternoon.
   hilding: jade, baggage. Cf. Dryden, *The Spanish Fryar,* II, iii: "How the
Gipsey answers me! Oh, 'tis a most notorious Hilding!"

pleasant. And you, ye staring hobby horse, what do you gaze at? Unbind me, you villain. Help him, you baggage, or I'll break thy bones.

CLARABELL. You can get * more, it seems, if you do, sir.

SWALLOW. Hold thy wicked tongue, or I will cut it out. 'Tis always wagging when it should not. Go seek out nurses, sirrha, for these unlucky bastards, whilst I pursue the 250 rogue that got them.   (*Exit* SWALLOW.

CLARABELL. I hope you will not scent him. Mark, is not this like the sire?

MARK. As 'twere spit out o'th' mouth on him.

CLARABELL. I wonder who are the dams of these puppies. They have somewhat of good faces besides Rightwit's.

MARK. He scorns, mistress, to leap an ugly jade, I dare swear.

CLARABELL. That which is next ye, take,
        And this I'll carry, for the father's sake.
                        (*Exeunt with children.*

Enter SIR GREGORY, MR. ZANY, *and their two men,* SPEAK *and* PLAINMAN.*

ZANY. Oh, *mounsiure* Plain: *très homble servaunt.** And what 260 news, in faith, from the roundhouse?

PLAINMAN. God's nownes, go look, thou ill-natur'd gull. I will tell thy mother o' all thy tricks when I come home.

ZANY. Be not so fierce, good Plain. I ha' done.

SPEAK. 'S precious— * Whose skin ha' ye got on? 'Tis none of your own. I'm sure I have seen it on some mangy fellow's back or other, if I could remember where.

SIR GREGORY. All's whole and sound as a bell under them. That's more than thou canst say, I dare take my oath.

get: beget; i.e., if he can still beget children, she is replaceable.
Enter . . . : The scene continues in the street.
mounsiure . . . : Zany's mocking adaptation of pseudo-French evidently indicates barbarous mispronunciation. The pronunciation "mounseer" is used from James Howard's *English Mounsieur* (1663) to W. S. Gilbert's *Ruddigore* (1887) as an expression of contempt.
'S precious: "By God's precious [blood]," a common oath.

Why thou hast been in Bridewell,* Speak. Prithee, what   270
went'st thou thither for? For picking a pocket, or cutting
a purse, man?

SPEAK. How, thou urchin?

SIR GREGORY. Nay, I perceive I have not lost money so often
but that somebody did somewhat.

SPEAK. I defy thee and thy damn'd dark sentences. If I
scourge thee not, hang me. (*Beats him.*)

PLAINMAN. Hold! God's nownes, thou hast no mercy. (*He
holds* SPEAK.)

SPEAK. Make a thief on me—

PLAINMAN (*to his master*). God's nownes, you should be so   280
us'd,* if you were but well serv'd.

ZANY. No, good Plain, thou art welcome from the roundhouse.

PLAINMAN. God's precious coals! *

ZANY. Nay, be not angry. Here's five shillings for thee.

PLAINMAN. Keep thy money, fool.

SIR GREGORY. Come, Mr. Zany, let us dine together at the
French ordinary.*

ZANY. With all my heart.

SPEAK. Faith, it is pity you two e'er should part.   (*Exeunt.*   290

Enter LORD COURTALL *and* SIR FRANCIS MAKELOVE.*

COURTALL. She is a pretty, gaysome, country thing: but the
all is, she has a very great fortune. Therefore, noble Sir

Bridewell: This famous prison, which housed all kinds of offenders, from
pickpockets and vagrants to prostitutes and debtors, was located two blocks
from the site of the Duke's Company's new Dorset Garden theatre.

us'd: treated.

God's precious coals: a meaningless, basically jocular oath. Cf. Charles II's
favorite, " 'od's fish."

the French ordinary: An ordinary is an eating house or tavern providing
public meals at a fixed price. The fools are probably proposing to dine at
Chatelin's or Lafronde's, fashionable French eating places in London. Pepys
reports visits to Chatelin's 13 March and 22 April 1668. The two houses are
linked in allusions in *Sir Martin Mar-all,* IV, i; *The Mulberry-Garden,* IV;
The Sullen Lovers, II; and *The Country Gentleman,* I.

Enter . . . . : The scene evidently continues in the street.

Francis, a word in the behalf of my brother, Jack Courtall. Your intimacy with her lady sister may much pro-
mote his suit.

MAKELOVE. You sure mistake, my lord, her fortune: for I have
heard Sir William Meanwell took the elder sister with
nothing.

COURTALL. Upon my honor, those that told you so did grossly
err, upon my knowledge. Will you oblige me by advanc-   300
ing this business?

MAKELOVE. Far as my life, command me.

COURTALL. Worthy Sir Francis, for this time I kiss your
hands.* And I beseech you remember, my brother wants
a wife that has money.   (*Exit.*

MAKELOVE. So do I:
       And if I find what ye have said be true,
       I for myself, not for a friend, must woo.   (*Exit.*

▼

Enter SWALLOW, MARK, *and* CLARABELL.*

SWALLOW. So Squire Rightwit, that noble gentleman, is
fast—fast as the jail can make him. And that heathenish,   310
vagabonding rogue, his companion Philario—I'll see
what a prison will do to tame him. Clarabell, I must to
Westminster.* Mark, if any inquire for me, it will be late
ere I come home. At eight tomorrow I shall be ready here
to receive any business.   (*Exit.*

CLARABELL. This ill-favor'd, condition'd * old fellow cares not
what mischief 'a does. As he goes out at one door, let us,
Mark, at another. I must needs see the poor prisoners.
                                  [MARK *hesitates.*]
Why stay'st thou?

    kiss your hands: a flowery and complimentary formula for bidding some-
one farewell (not an implicit stage direction).
    Enter . . . : Swallow's house, early afternoon.
    Westminster: site of the law courts where Swallow presumably has busi-
ness.
    ill-favor'd, condition'd: ugly and bad-tempered.

MARK. But are you so mad, mistress, to go to the jail? Faith,   320
you'll hardly find one in ten thousand of your mind. But
to what prison are they committed? That you do not
know.

CLARABELL. Pox on't! I was so dismay'd with the ill news, I
rememb'red not to inform myself.

MARK. Never chafe. I will discover their abode to you.

CLARABELL. Oh, excellent Mark: thou art the better genius
of thy sex.   (*Exit ambo.*

▼

Enter at one door LORD COURTALL, *at another* SIR GREGORY
and SPEAK.*

COURTALL. Sir Gregory—most fortunately met. I heard you
were in town and was going to inquire you out; but my   330
labor is happily prevented.

SIR GREGORY. I am glad to see your lordship in health.

COURTALL. Shall we in to the Fleece * and congratulate
yours, and remember our friends in the country in a
glass of sack?

SIR GREGORY. Faith, my lord, I have almost forsworn coming
into a tavern since I was last most barbarously pawn'd
at one by a company of villainous sharks for the reckoning.

SPEAK (*aside*). Ah, thou great calf! Thou mun need bleat out
all, to make thy sen * hooted at when we come home   340
into the country. Ah—

COURTALL. I hope, sir, you know me better than to suspect
me to serve you such a heathenish trick. I pray you, let
us enter.

SIR GREGORY. Your lordship's to command.   (*Exeunt.*

▼

    Enter . . . : the street, midafternoon.
    the Fleece: There were several taverns with this name in London; see de
Castro's "Dictionary." The reference here is probably to the one in Bridges
Street mentioned by Aubrey.
    sen: self (dialect).

RIGHTWIT *and* PHILARIO *as in prison.* * *To them,* CLARABELL.

CLARABELL. Give you joy, gentlemen, of your fine quarters!
    What say you now to a score of wenches, or a fresh tav-
    ern frolic, ha? How like an ass thou look'st, Rightwit.
    How is't, Philario?
PHILARIO. Bad enough, of all conscience.   350
RIGHTWIT. What the Devil brought thee hither?
CLARABELL. Things call'd legs—with a willing mind. I
    thought a woman would have been welcome to you, but
    I perceive you know not what to do with one. Fare ye
    well.
RIGHTWIT. Stay, I can cure thy greensickness * yet, as low as
    the tide is.   (CLARABELL *sings.*)

Song

If I were tortur'd with greensickness,
Dost think I would be cur'd by thee?
I then too soon might swell in thickness—   360
A pox upon your remedy!
The cure may prove worse than the anguish,
And I of a fresh disease might languish.
But I'll keep myself from such distemper
In spite of all that you dare do;
Although you are so free to venter, *
I'll be hang'd if I did not baffle you.

RIGHTWIT. Nay, like enough. Come, prithee let me kiss thee
    a little. 'Tis that, I know, thou cam'st for. The holiest of
    you cannot live without it. (*She laughs and sings again.*) 370

prison: probably a bailiff's house where debtors were confined. The gentry
lodged in private quarters, others in the "common" side of the house. The
time is now midafternoon.
    greensickness: chlorosis, a form of aenemia once common in adolescent
girls, which made them so pale they looked "green." Marriage and childbear-
ing allegedly cured it—hence the popular meaning, "longing for sex."
    venter: venture (obsolete or dialectal form). The author may be making an
awkward pun on "venter" in its sense as a noun: one of two or more women
who bear offspring to the same man.

Kissing's not such a recreation
But, faith and troth, I can live without it.
Though I confess 'tis all in fashion
And so will continue, we need not doubt it.
Though many a cuckold, I am certain,
Hath been made by kissing—and their fortune.
But to Heaven all cuckolds go, 'tis granted; *
Therefore my husband's soul I'll save:
Of horns he never shall be scanted,
Whilst I but youth and courage have.   380

RIGHTWIT. Good, but whither must the cuckold-makers go, I
prithee?
CLARABELL. Why, to Heaven too: it is a meritorious act to
save a soul, and without question we shall be sav'd, not
damn'd, for such admirable charity.
PHILARIO. Rare doctrine! You preach well.

To them, MARK, *disguis'd.*

MARK. Now, now, now's the time! I have treppan'd * all the
people of the house out of the way that are on this side,
except the Turnkey and a relation of mine of the weaker
sex, that has given me leave to bind her, if I see oc-   390
casion, with her master. The tapster is gone to his father's funeral with his mistress and others of the family.
The master have I sent a porter for to meet a special
friend of his at Westminster.* If you have brain enough
ere he return without an uproar to make your party good
with the Turnkey (for fear he raise the common side)
you may off as clear as a whistle.*

to Heaven all cuckolds go: A proverbial consolation, cited a number of
times in comedies of the late seventeenth century—for example, in Act IV of
Otway's *The Souldiers Fortune* and in Act II of Congreve's *Love for Love.*
treppan'd: tricked.
The master . . . at Westminster: To get the master of the prison out of the
way, Mark has sent him a false message from someone for whom he would
be sure to wait.
off clear as a whistle: proverbial, though usually "clean" as a whistle. Obviously a dirty whistle does not work.

PHILARIO. Pox, can'st thou not make him drunk?

MARK. He scorns to be overcome with the Creature.* He is a
holy Brother.*   400

RIGHTWIT. 'S death, I'll down and beat out the rogue's brains
with his bunch of keys. That's a safe and sure way—

CLARABELL. To be hang'd. Does your neck itch for a rope? I
have a safer way, by far, than that. As my humour is
comical, so shall my exploits be. If I free you not without
a tragedy, condemn me.

RIGHTWIT. Dear rogue, thou cam'st to free us, then.

CLARABELL. But how? Can you tell? No brains, betwixt you
both. Here—clap on these false beards to disguise your
true rogueries. I will go work with the Turnkey; and   410
when I give the watchword, come down. I'll whisper it to
you. Mark, be ready for your business. I'll bring you off
clearly, except you spoil yourselves by the way for fear.

(Exeunt severally.

▼

Enter CLARABELL *with the* TURNKEY *below;* * RIGHTWIT *and*
PHILARIO, *as unseen, above.*

RIGHTWIT. I shall admire her wit if she can cheat our diligent
officer. Philario, attend the sequel. See where they enter.

CLARABELL. I have been giving my kinsmen counsel: to bear
their captivity with patience, and those afflictions that
the Lord for their offenses has visited them withal.

TURNKEY [*aside*]. A virtuous woman. I do not believe but she
is a Sister, and one that stands up for the Cause.*   420

CLARABELL. Here, Brother, is a mite for ye.* And the Lord put

the Creature: humorous term for intoxicating liquor.
holy Brother: a puritan.
Enter . . . : a different part of the prison, though the set probably remains the same. Rightwit and Philario presumably enter "above" in the first
balcony on the side where they exited; Clarabell and the Turnkey could play
against the proscenium on the opposite side, using a proscenium door for the
closet in which she locks him.
the Cause: the puritan cause.
Here, Brother, is a mite for ye: Clarabell tips the Turnkey.

it in thy heart to look upon the poor prisoners with an eye of pity.

TURNKEY. For your sake I shall do much, for I perceive you are a Sister in the Lord.

CLARABELL [aside]. I shall go near to spoil all with laughing.

RIGHTWIT [above, to Philario]. A brave wench! She would make an admirable comedian. I cannot yet comprehend her design.

CLARABELL. I pray thee, Brother, fetch them some wine. The   430
while will I look for money to pay for the same. "Give wine to the afflicted and to him that is of heavy heart. Aye, let him drink and remember his misery no more." Proverbs, chapter 30, verse 7.*

TURNKEY. 'Tis so set down in Holy Writ.

(He unlocks a door, as to fetch wine. She locks him in, and catches up his keys, and opens another door.)

CLARABELL [calling upstairs]. Halloo!

Enter RIGHTWIT, PHILARIO, and MARK. They all run out, locking the doors after them. The TURNKEY pounds and knocks within.

TURNKEY. Sister? Why, Sister, open, in the name of the Lord——Sister, thou hast not beguil'd me? Oh, oh, oh. It is even so. And here will I lie and mourn in a holy si-   440
lence for thy fraud.

(Scene alters.)

▼

Enter CLARABELL, RIGHTWIT, PHILARIO, and MARK.*

CLARABELL. So now shift for yourselves. I think I have done my part.

"Give wine to the afflicted . . .": The correct citation is chapter 31, verses 6–7.

Enter . . . . : the street, immediately afterward.

RIGHTWIT. And I'll do mine: I cannot but marry thee for this
good turn.

CLARABELL. I mean not to marry with any man; but when I
am weary of my life, I'll have thee. Meantime, go get my
father's good will, and I'm a rogue if I marry thee not as
soon as thou hast it. (*All laugh.*)

RIGHTWIT. As I have a soul, it shall be the third and last thing
I'll do today. First I'll go home. Secondly I'll shift me.*   450
Thirdly I will go to thy father, and if I get not his good
will, despise me.

CLARABELL. If thou dost, I will adore thee.

PHILARIO. Thou art not mad? To go to jail again, and be
whipp'd and fetter'd for out-running it now?

MARK. I hope not. 'S wounds, my master will give you his
soul before his daughter.

RIGHTWIT. Let the Devil take that: he has most right to 't. I'll
have the wench, and he shall give her me freely.

CLARABELL. Make this good, and I am thine.* Otherwise I   460
will never see thy face again.

RIGHTWIT. Once more I swear I'll do 't.

CLARABELL. Adieu, till I see you at our house at night,
ha, ha, ha.   (*Exeunt* CLARABELL *and* MARK.

RIGHTWIT. Well, well. Long as ye list,* laugh on. Advance,
Philario. I will home.   (*Exeunt.*

[End of Act IV]

shift me: change clothes.

I'll have the wench . . . I am thine: Rightwit and Clarabell enter here into
what technically is a bilateral oral contract before a witness. Should Clarabell
decline to marry Rightwit after he has completed his end of the agreement
(if he can), he could sue her for breach of contract with some hope of collect-
ing monetary damages, or at least of recovering any money he might have
spent in fulfilling his part of the bargain.

list: please.

ACT THE FIFTH

Enter RIGHTWIT, *disguis'd; to him,* MARK.*

RIGHTWIT. Is the Counsellor at home?
MARK. He's in his study, sir.

Enter CLARABELL.

CLARABELL. What would this gentleman?
MARK. Some words,* madam, with my master.
CLARABELL. Here comes my father, sir.   (*Exit* CLARABELL.

Enter SWALLOW.

RIGHTWIT [*aside*]. The rascal knows me not!
SWALLOW. Is your business to me?
RIGHTWIT. It is; and I should let you know 't in private.
SWALLOW. Here is not any but my clerk. Him may we trust
    with any concern.   10
RIGHTWIT. I come for counsel, and of you will purchase it at
    any rate you please. In earnest, here's two pieces.
SWALLOW. In all that you desire, command.
RIGHTWIT. There is betwixt a rich and wealthy heiress and
    myself some love. I fain would have her, though my for-
    tune never can deserve her. And know, her friends will
    be so much against our match, that I by stealth must

Enter . . . : Swallow's office. Almost 6 P.M.
words: added by the editors. See the Textual Notes.

marry her. Now, I would know what danger may attend
the theft, of stealing * such a wife.

SWALLOW. There have been laws most rigorous against it.*   20
But if the lady loves you, slip with her to some church at
a convenient hour, provide a parson and a brace of witnesses, and let your mistress lead you * by the hand and
the church enter first. So shall the law (if any follow it
against you) conclude that she stole you, and not you
her. So will their loves in time embrace you. For the
present, you may smile and fear not the worst that they
can act against you.

MARK (aside). I wonder who this is.

RIGHTWIT. Here's something more for your good counsel.   30
And to endear me farther to you, you shall not deny
(because I would not make a public business on 't), to
give my bride, and be our father, as the custom is. I
would not make but few that know me too much acquainted with it, for fear by any cross mischance it
might be thwarted.

SWALLOW. Your place and hour, and I'll infallibly attend you.

RIGHTWIT. St. Dunstan's Church in Fleet Street,* about four
i'th' morning.* Now 'tis almost six.

theft . . . stealing: By these terms Rightwit means that the marriage must
be "clandestine," not that it will involve abduction or duress.

laws most rigorous against it: Use of force or coercion in "stealing" an
heiress was a felony. The relevant statutes are 3 Hen. VII, c.2, and 29 Eliz.
c.9. Offenders could be hanged—and sometimes were. See, for example,
Joseph Keble, *Reports in the Court of Kings Bench* (1685), III, 193, for a
death sentence carried out in 1673. Swallow's advice is based on the assumption that the woman is entirely willing.

let your mistress lead you . . . : This advice, though not referring to any
particular law, has legal point. Forcible abduction or duress would be
grounds for declaring the marriage legally void. By having the bride demon-
strate her willingness before the "brace of witnesses" Swallow advises,
Rightwit can probably invalidate the most obvious way of proceeding against
the marriage. By #105 of the Canons of 1603 the evidence of such witnesses
would be freely admissible in a church court.

St. Dunstan's Church in Fleet Street: "Adjoining to *Clifford's Inn lane,*
and fronting *Fleetstreet,* is St. *Dunstane's* Church . . . a good handsome
Freestone Building, with a fair Dial hanging over into the Street" (Strype's
Stow, pt. 3, p. 276). Properly known as St. Dunstan's in the West, the church
remains in use to the present day.

about four i'th' morning: This is highly irregular: Canon 62 forbade the

SWALLOW. I will go sup; and in my clothes I'll sleep, till   40
    toward the hour, because I will be ready without trouble.
RIGHTWIT. I am oblig'd to you and will requite your kindness.
                  (Claps a paper in MARK's *hand and exits.*
SWALLOW. What was't the gentleman put into your hand?
MARK. A shilling, sir.
SWALLOW. He is very noble.   *(Exit* SWALLOW.
                              (MARK *reads.*)

Enter CLARABELL.

CLARABELL. Now what are you reading?
MARK. A sad sentence: Rightwit in some odd quarrel is
    wounded almost to death, and begs to breathe his latest
    words into your ear before he dies.
CLARABELL. Hang him; this is some trick, because he could   50
    not make good his word (as 'twas impossible, indeed, he
    should), to get me by my father's will. I'll not come at
    him.
MARK. If he had perform'd it, you would sooner have laughed
    at him than requited him.
CLARABELL. The very act would have made me dote on him;
    and as I promis'd, I would have done. But his foolish
    promise of what he knew he never could, or durst offer
    to effect, makes me hate him.
MARK. If I can prove he has effected all he swore to you at   60
    your last parting, you'll stand to your bargain?
CLARABELL. Yes, faith, will I.
MARK. I'll have a chair * (by that time that my master has
    supp'd and lain down one half hour) to carry ye where I,
    clear as the day, will make apparent all is done that
    gallant Rightwit promis'd.

---

celebration of marriage except between the hours of 8 A.M. and noon. Marriage at other hours was technically illegal, though the illegality did not af-
fect the validity of the marriage. For a further discussion, see the Appendix.
    a chair: a sedan chair, an early form of taxi. It was a closed conveyance
which seated one person, carried on two poles by a pair of bearers, one in
front and one behind.

CLARABELL. Why didst thou tell me he was wounded? To ter-
    rify me?
MARK. With your bright eyes, he is; with nothing else, no
    other weapons; and those are sharp enough.   70
CLARABELL. But this can never be, that thou hast told me.
MARK. I'll make you, your own sweet self, confess it is. But
    hark, what noise?

Enter SWALLOW *and a* MESSENGER.

SWALLOW [*to Messenger*]. Rightwit and Philario fled the
    prison? The Devil fly away with them! Leave me tonight.
    I will tomorrow farther inform my self of their escape.
                                    (*Exit* MESSENGER.
    Clarabell, to bed. And Mark, you had best to see your
    chamber too.
MARK. Shall I not wait you abroad at the appointed hour?
SWALLOW. No. I have sent to Newman, my next neighbor, to   80
    be ready with his coach. Take you rest.
CLARABELL [*aside*]. I thought there would be an alarum.
                                    (*Exeunt.*

▼

Enter LORD COURTALL, LADY MEANWELL, PROCREATE, *and*
MISTRESS FAITH.*

COURTALL [*to Procreate*]. Madam, I cannot work * this fool to
    anything of your concern. He is in love with the rich
    counsellor's daughter.

Enter RIGHTWIT [*unseen, during the following speech*].

PROCREATE. If by my advice and policy you have effected all
    your wishes,* and what's worth all, brought Sir Francis

    Enter . . . : The setting could be either the street or the Meanwells'
rooms in Rightwit's house. Using the street would eliminate an extra scene
change at V, 136.1. The time is 6 P.M.
    work: persuade, manipulate.
    all your wishes: i.e., she has helped him seduce Faith.

to your bay to marry Mistress Faith—hang me if I do not
spoil the wedding, if you answer not my expectation and
your own promises.   90

RIGHTWIT. Faith, and do, madam, if they do not handsome
things by you, that have so well deserved of them.

COURTALL. This is an uncivil interruption.

RIGHTWIT. 'Twill be advantageous to you all, if you will give
me leave to be an actor in your business. Mistress Faith
is my cousin. She has been kind and good natur'd to
your lordship: * your lordship would requite her. One
good turn merits another. The French mademoiselle
wants a recompense for doing the better part of those
two that belong to her nation, which is "bawding" in our   100
mother tongue. (The other is poxing, and much worse.)
I'll bring your designs to perfection, if you'll all be rul'd
by me, yet, ere day; and mine own, too. So please to let
my service excuse my "uncivil interruption."

COURTALL. Since you are so well acquainted with our affairs,
we shall not decline your assistance.

RIGHTWIT [to Mistress Faith]. Madam, Sir Francis Makelove,
I perceive, in a heat of hot and violent expectation of that
which ne'er will be, will shackle with you with a wet
finger.* The venerable French matron wants one of the   110
country gentlemen, both which, indeed, are rivals in the
love of Swallow's daughter (which loves neither of
them). Now if you, Cousin Faith, appoint Sir Francis—or
my lady Procreate here procure him for you—to wait you
at some new-fashion'd mumming dance, or French
frolic, let me alone to bring the two country men.

[To Procreate] One you shall have, if you please to step
over to St. Dunstan's. The other I have chosen for another friend.

PROCREATE. I'll have a French ball at my house, and all   120
things ready, in a trice.

kind and good natur'd to your lordship: a euphemism for sexually compliant.

with a wet finger: readily, without hesitation. The phrase carries a vulgar
connotation, but apparently not an obscene one.

COURTALL. What hour is't?

PROCREATE. Just six. I'll send for Makelove.

RIGHTWIT. Expect the country gentlemen of me. But look you get handsome disguises: your chosen lover must take you for another, madam, till he has ta'en you for good and all.

PROCREATE. I warrant you. I'll but set things in order and be ready.

LADY MEANWELL. Cousin Rightwit, we had rare fortune to   130
have you our counsellor.

RIGHTWIT. Aye, madam, you could not have lighted eas'ly of such another rascal to advance your designs. No words—away, dispatch! 'Tis o're-turn'd six.

COURTALL. Heaven sent ye to us in a happy hour.

RIGHTWIT. Against your wills I was your counsellor.

(*Exeunt severally.*

▼

Enter again RIGHTWIT, *and* SIR GREGORY.*

RIGHTWIT. Noble Sir Gregory?

SIR GREGORY [*aside*]. This fellow is a conjurer. Now will the rogue beat me into nothing, for serving him as he had served me (if I had not prevented him, with Zany's   140
help). He deals with the Devil and has laid a circle, out of which magical compass he will not suffer me to stir. He could never light on me else, as he does everywhere thus. I must speak to him.

[*To Rightwit*] Noble Mr. Rightwit, accept this diamond and forgive my last bad usage of you. I protest, that codshead,* Zany, enforc'd me to join with him in the abuse. But—

RIGHTWIT. Upon your penitence, I forgive it. And for this jewel I'm your debtor, but will owe you nothing before   150
day, if you please. Therefore know there is a masquing dance at the French lady's in the Strand, out of which

Enter . . . : The scene changes to or continues in the street.
codshead: obnoxious fool, blockhead.

there will be some brides stol'n tonight. Zany is to snap young Mistress Swallow out amongst the rest, whom by a known disguise he will find out. Ye deserve her better than he.

SIR GREGORY. I would give a hundred pound to baffle him.

RIGHTWIT. Go, fit you with a handsome antic habit, and I will warrant you she's yours, if you'll be rul'd by me.

SIR GREGORY. I'll to the Master of the Wardrobe of one of the   160
playhouses and procure what ye speak of immediately.*

RIGHTWIT. Away, then.   (*Exeunt severally.*

Enter MAKELOVE,* *brave.*

MAKELOVE. I must shift myself. And in the dance Procreate has sent me word of, I shall (in spite of my politic Lord), get Mistress Faith, in my disguise, away to Dunstan's, as my ingenious Frenchwoman has plotted it. And when I have her, I may justly claim a cow's grass in Heaven,* and tell the people there, if they already know it not, I have kiss'd both the sisters, the incomparable sisters! Yet will I watch my wife if I can, for having a trick of the sis-   170
ter.   (*Exit.*

Enter at another door, RIGHTWIT *and* ZANY. ZANY *slinks back.**

RIGHTWIT. No flinching, Mr. Zany.

ZANY. The darkness of the night eclips'd you from my knowledge—
    [*Aside*] I shake and tremble like an aspen leaf, all over, for pure fear. He will be horribly reveng'd on me for the

Master of the Wardrobe . . . immediately: The theatres had endless dif-
ficulties in trying to keep costumes intact and on the premises. Private use of
costumes was forbidden (see, for example, Public Record Office LC 5/141,
p. 307), but for a small gratuity even an outsider like Sir Gregory could probably wangle a loan.
    Enter . . . . : The scene continues in the street, during the evening.
    claim a cow's grass in Heaven: The origin and precise meaning of this
striking phrase have escaped us.
    Enter at another door . . . . : The scene continues, still later that evening.

trick the knight and I put upon him about the children. Would I were in a wilderness alone.

RIGHTWIT. Sir, a word. (*Whispers him.*)

ZANY. Worthy Mr. Rightwit! Accomplish this, and I am your   180
slave eternally.

(*Aside*) I was afraid he would have swing'd * me, but the fear is over.

RIGHTWIT. Nay, no trifling, Mr. Zany, but about your business. At the Frenchwoman's, slip in amongst the rest, and I will farther direct you.

ZANY. I am gone, I am gone.   (*Exeunt severally.*

▼

Enter LADY MEANWELL *and* MISTRESS FAITH *and* PROCREATE.*

LADY MEANWELL. I must acquaint my husband, or I may not go. But here he comes—

[*Enter* MEANWELL.]

Dear Meanwell, will you see a little admirable French   190
dancing tonight at Lady Procreate's? She is in person come to have us to her house. I pray thee, let us go.

PROCREATE. Yes, good Sir William. Let us have the honor of your presence.

MEANWELL. How, madam? Go from home at this wicked hour, when nothing that is good's abroad?

LADY MEANWELL (*aside*). You will spoil my sister's fortune.

MEANWELL (*aside*). This night work * can never honorably prefer her.

LADY MEANWELL [*aside*]. It must be done by policy, more   200
than niceness. This night will complete the business.

MEANWELL [*aside*]. Upon that score, for once I'll break my resolution.

---

swing'd: beaten.
Enter . . . : the Meanwells' lodging, very late at night.
night work: literally, late-night socializing, but Meanwell gives it an unsavory connotation.

[*To Procreate*] Madam, your never-to-be-equall'd
goodness obliges me thus late, to leave my lodging to
wait upon you.

PROCREATE. I'll study, sir, to merit the honor ye vouchsafe
me.   (*Exeunt.*

▼

Enter MARK, *and* CLARABELL *in a sedan.**

MARK. So, chairmen, down with your load at this door. There
is your money. [*Pays them.*]   (*Exeunt sedan carriers.*   210

Enter RIGHTWIT.

RIGHTWIT. Who's there?
MARK. A friend or twain.
RIGHTWIT. Thou hast brought Clarabell?
CLARABELL. No—
RIGHTWIT. Thou liest—
CLARABELL. The sedan did, indeed. Therefore thou liest. But
wherefore am I brought hither?
RIGHTWIT. 'Tis most convenient for many reasons. Some of
them I will give thee; take them in thy ear. (*Whispers.*)
In, Mark, in. I hear a hurry of coaches. Hither they come.   220
(*Exeunt.*

▼

Enter PROCREATE, LORD COURTALL, SIR WILLIAM MEANWELL,
LADY MEANWELL, MISTRESS FAITH, *and others.**

PROCREATE. Gallants, you are all most welcome. I want words
to express my sense of the honor that you do me in grac-
ing my poor house with your rich presence. A while I
must beg ye to entertain yourselves.   (*Exit* PROCREATE.
(*Music above a while.*)

Enter . . . : The Strand, outside Procreate's house. This scene would
probably have been acted against the proscenium. The time is the early
hours of the morning.
Enter . . . : The remainder of the action takes place in Procreate's house.

Enter six PAGES *bearing torches,*
with vizards *
upon their faces and
wreaths of rosemary and bays on their heads.
After them,
SIR FRANCIS MAKELOVE *leading* MISTRESS FAITH,
both disguis'd in masquing habits.

MEANWELL. What are these? French antics?
LADY MEANWELL. They are the gallants of the town, in masquing habits.

Enter CLARABELL, PROCREATE, *and* LEONORA
like nymphs,
but vizards on their faces.
RIGHTWIT *and two more* * *enter, disguis'd.*
They choose out their women and dance.

MEANWELL. This sight was worth seeing.
LADY MEANWELL. And yet ye would scarce be gotten abroad.

Music plays
and they dance again a while;
then off the stage severally, in couples.

MEANWELL. They are all vanish'd.   230
LADY MEANWELL. They will return, straight.

Enter SPEAK *and* PLAINMAN.

SPEAK. The doors being open, we made bold to come in, hearing the fiddles—to look for a couple of strene * country

---

vizards: masks. Such a mask could be mounted on a stick to be held in the hand, or could be attached directly to the wearer's headgear—as was presumably the case here, since the bearers are already carrying torches. The association of vizards with prostitutes was already common, but they were not yet nearly so disreputable as they were to become.

RIGHTWIT *and two more:* i.e., Zany and Sir Gregory.

strene: The author may just mean "strayed," or she may be trying to use a participial form of the obsolete verb "strene" (to copulate) as an adjective, in which case she means something like "lecherous."

gentlemen, believing this place had ta'en 'um up. But I
con see neither sign nor token on them.

PLAINMAN. God's nownes, here's brave sport! See thee here,
Speak—mummers, mummers!

*Enter the torchbearers, two by two,
and all that danc'd out,* SWALLOW *following.*
MAKELOVE *pulls [off his vizard, and* MISTRESS FAITH *hers.]*

MAKELOVE. Your pardon, brother Meanwell, and yours, best
sister, for stealing of a wedding without your knowledge.
I took my mistress whilst she and Fortune were in the   24(
good humour.

MEANWELL. I wish you happiness and am proud of your alli-
ance.

COURTALL [*unmasking*]. Married, Sir Francis?

MAKELOVE. Good my lord, are you here? Forgive me. Love is
the noblest cheat that is. I fear'd your brother might
have slipp'd in favor before me.

COURTALL. What must be, must be. Sir I wish you joy.
(*Laughs aside*) Ha, ha, ha. Now the work's done.

SIR GREGORY [*unmasking*]. Mr. Zany, you are baffled. Here is   25(
the counsellor's daughter.

SWALLOW. How!

SIR GREGORY. Show thy face, sweetest. Nothing now can part
us.

PROCREATE [*unmasking*]. No indeed, Sir Gregory—nothing
upon earth now.

SIR GREGORY. What the murrain!* Thou scurvy, sodden,
French hag. Dost think to baffle me? I never meant to
have thee, by this light.

ZANY [*unmasking*]. No swaggering, Sir Gregory. Here is the   260
bride you aim'd at: mine, fast as the priest could make
her.*

What the murrain: in this form, a meaningless imprecation. A murrain is
an epizootic disease in cattle: to wish a murrain *on* someone is to wish a
plague on him.

I never meant to have thee . . . fast as the priest could make he: These
tricked marriages are, in fact, not legally valid. *Error Personae* "is not only

LEONORA [*unmasking*]. Yes, here are witnesses enow, Mr. Zany.

ZANY. Here's brave juggling! Rightwit, that rogue, has cheated us both. The Devil take him.

RIGHTWIT [*unmasking*]. Sir, your blessing.

SWALLOW. Blessing? What's here? Rightwit!

CLARABELL [*unmasking*]. Yes indeed, and Clarabell too.

SWALLOW. Have I given away my only daughter to the only   270
man I hate? I dream, sure!

RIGHTWIT. No, you wake, and your eyes are open enough to see how you are over-reach'd, lawyer, by your own law.

SWALLOW. Thou art a cunning, wicked, unthrift, and thou shalt not have her, for all this.

CLARABELL. His title is too good for you,* sir, to cut off his interest, I assure you.

SWALLOW. Thou wert ever a pert, headstrong baggage.

COURTALL. No chafing, now, Mr. Swallow. He is a gentleman and wants nothing to rank him with the best, but means.   280
He is my kinsman, and I daresay by his future carriage he will deserve your love.

MEANWELL. He is, by marriage, my near relation too; and of a private family.* There's few can boast themselves of better blood. I pray you, sir, receive him as your son: for so the law of Heaven on earth has made him.

SIR GREGORY. They are all baffled as well as we, Mr. Zany.

ZANY. So it seems. Brother Rightwit, much joy to thee. I'm glad now it was my chance to have thy sister.

RIGHTWIT. Make much on her, Isaac. She's a good wench.   290

---

an Impediment to a Marriage Contract, but it even dissolves the Contract it self, through a defect of Consent in the Person contracting" (John Ayliffe, *Parergon juris canonici Anglicani* [1726], pp. 362–363). As is customary in Restoration comedy, however, the marriages are allowed to stand. For an excellent discussion of conventions in the comedies and the laws involved, see Gellert Spencer Alleman, *Matrimonial Law and the Materials of Restoration Comedy* (Wallingford, Pa.: privately printed, 1942), pp. 60–72.

thou shalt not have her. . . . His title is too good for you . . . : Swallow is probably without legal recourse—as he himself soon admits, "there's no remedy." For a discussion of the legal questions involved, see the Appendix.

private family: a family occupying its own house—i.e., one with inherited property rather than one which has made its money in trade.

ZANY. As on my soul.

PROCREATE. Droop not, Sir Gregory. The French mademoiselle can love de English man with as much passion as
your country ladies can the monsieur.

SIR GREGORY. Spoken like a kind rascal. I'll learn to love thee
as well as I can, for my heart.

MAKELOVE. Mr. Swallow, you will not be the only man in-
ex'rable today?

SWALLOW. Since there's no remedy: for my lord's sake, Sir
William Meanwell's, and yours, I receive him to my 300
arms—with a hope he will leave his unthrifty course.

(Embraces him.)

RIGHTWIT. I'll clasp thy daughter fast in mine, and she shall
live within my bosom still.

MARK. All's well that end's well.

MEANWELL. Sirrha Ralph!

RALPH. Your pleasure?

MEANWELL. From this day forward, I disclaim you for my servant. You shall breed no more dissension 'twixt me and
my wife.

[*To the company*] This rogue had almost persuaded me 310
to a divorce * from my lady, had not her virtue prov'd itself above his envy.

[*To Ralph*] Sir, pray be gone. Before this whole congregation, I discharge you my service.

RALPH. There are none but fools but will be knaves.* God be
with you, sir.

[*Aside*] But that wish is vain.

divorce: As the term is used in the twentieth century, divorce was not really possible. The first instance in England (Henry VIII excluded) in which a
man was allowed to remarry following separation *a mensa et thoro* occurred
in 1670 when Parliament passed a bill allowing Lord Roos to remarry in
order to prevent the extinction of his peerage. Hence the subject was topical.
Divorce as such became possible only about 1700, but long remained prohib-
itively difficult and expensive. What Meanwell has in mind is what we would
call legal separation.

none but fools but will be knaves: a sententious twist on the old saw—but
one with real satiric bite in this situation.

[*To Meanwell*] Heaven will always be on your side, I'll
make it appear at our farewell (if you will deign to hear
me) by an old proverb.   320

MEANWELL. Aye, I prithee, let's have the fruits on't at part-
ing.

RALPH (*sings*).

O Cuckold, thou of men most bless'd;
O Cuckold, thou of chosen nation; *
Fate's self has given thee on thy crest
Sure tokens of salvation.*
The horns that do thy head invest
Are proof against damnation.

MEANWELL. Away with thee and thy ill-favor'd proverbs—
(*Draws.*)   (*Exit* RALPH.

COURTALL. Much joy unto ye all! At my own charge, I'll   330
crown your nuptials with a noble feast today. In the
meantime we'll celebrate the pleasure of them in a
sprightly dance in grace of Hymen.

(*They all dance.*)

PLAINMAN. God's nownes, we'll have a Lonkashire hornpipe,*
friend Speak!
[*To the music*] Strike up, you infidels. Oh, brave!

ZANY. I am married, Plain, as well as the rest.

PLAINMAN. Yea, yea; afore ye ha' wit.

SIR GREGORY. And I have a wife, too.

SPEAK. Two? You'll e'en have enough o' one, I warrant you!   340
[*To the music*] Once more, I say, strike up.

(*They two dance a jig.*)

COURTALL. Once more I wish a general happiness.

of chosen nation: added by the editors to fill a hiatus.
salvation: a play on the proverb "all cuckolds go to Heaven."
Lonkashire hornpipe: A hornpipe is a vigorous country dance, later to be
particularly associated with the merrymaking of sailors. Wales, Derbyshire,
and Lancashire developed particular forms of this dance.

[*Aside*] And may all that kind mistresses enjoy requite
them as I have done mine today.

PHILARIO. All that Philario can conclude to say,
Is that he will go drink healths without delay.

[*Exeunt omnes.*

[End of Act V]

Finis

APPENDIX
A NOTE ON MARRIAGE LAW

For information on this subject the reader may consult Thomas Poynter, *A Concise View of the Doctrine and Practice of the Ecclesiastical Courts in Doctors' Commons, on Various Points Relative to the Subject of Marriage and Divorce,* 2d ed. (London: J. & W. T. Clarke, 1824); Leonard Shelford, *A Practical Treatise of the Law of Marriage and Divorce* (Philadelphia: Littell, 1841); Nevill Geary, *The Law of Marriage and Family Relations* (London: Adam and Charles Black, 1892); and Gellert Spencer Alleman, *Matrimonial Law and the Materials of Restoration Comedy* (Wallingford, Pa.: privately printed, 1942).

There are five basic grounds of possible legal objection to the marriage of Rightwit and Clarabell. None, however, appears to constitute the basis for a serious challenge to the validity of the marriage.

(1) Abduction or duress. Since Clarabell is willing, the only issue is proving that she was so. This is the point of Swallow's advice that Rightwit provide a "brace of witnesses" to watch her lead him into the church.

(2) If Clarabell is under the age of twenty-one she must have her parents' consent (Canon #100). The author does not specify Clarabell's age. But even if she is not of age, Swallow's participation in the ceremony makes this a questionable ground for a suit in nullity. He has, after all, given away his daughter, and a suit would be challenged on the principle *volenti non fit injuria,* both because he willfully

139

gave away a woman who turned out to be his daughter, and because he willfully devised a scheme to defy the requirement of parental consent. See Geary, pp. 229 ff., and Shelford, p. 333.

(3) If Swallow can show a "specific interest"—in this case, that he will have to support his daughter and any children who result from the marriage—then he is entitled to bring suit in the ecclesiastical courts to annul the marriage of his child (see Shelford, p. 334). Here Rightwit's poverty could be a legal liability, though if Clarabell has money of her own such a suit could not be maintained. But even if she does not, the courts would not be likely to dissolve a marriage contracted and consummated by happily wedded adults.

(4) No banns have been read, as is required unless the marriage is performed by special license, and (5) the ceremony takes place outside the canonical hours. On both grounds the marriage is technically illegal, but as Alleman observes of such cases, "the fact that the ceremony was illegal had nothing whatever to do with its validity," and "the courts might punish the man, the priest, the witnesses, and the accessories, but they could not dissolve the union thus created" (pp. 34, 59). The point of Canon 62, requiring intent of marriage to be "published three several Sundays or holy days" in advance, was to warn parents of minors of surreptitious marriages, and generally to render any clandestine marriage difficult. But canon law punished the minister, not the couple, for violation of this requirement. The same held true for marriages out of canonical hours: the laity were not bound (see Poynter, p. 81). The punishments for violating these rules could be quite severe, but in practice private chaplains and venal clergymen did so with great frequency. Certain London churches—St. Dunstan's not among them—were noted for their ministers' willingness to perform irregular marriages (see Alleman, chap. 2, esp. pp. 47–49).

In sum, Swallow has essentially no hope of successfully challenging the validity of the marriage his daughter has contracted. His final acquiescence to the marriage is, however, of more than sentimental importance. He can certainly disinherit his daughter (as parents in Restoration comedies so often threaten to do), even if he must provide her and her children the necessities of life. And the common law courts could refuse dower to a woman whose marriage was clandestine. Even the consent of the woman made no difference if she was under sixteen—as is the heroine of Wycherley's *Gentleman Dancing-Master,* for example. By law (4 and 5 Ph. & Mary, c.8) her next of kin could enjoy her estate during her lifetime, and after her death the property descended as if she had never lived. For the most part, however, Restoration comedies ignore the technicalities or treat them very lightly. In this respect the cavalier handling of marriage law in *The Frolicks* is quite typical of other plays from this time.

TEXTUAL NOTES

The following notes give the manuscript reading in all instances of
substantive emendation. They also record the writer's use of inferior
brackets, repetitions, cancellations, and other peculiarities. Notes
are keyed to line numbers enumerated consecutively through each
act. Stage directions are not counted in the lineation. We have followed the convention by which 42.1 refers to the first line of a stage
direction following line 42, and so forth.

Dedication

10   ⌊*fame great Sir*⌋
12   *this* written twice
14   scribal blot before *splendid*
15   *heaven* ⌊*the sun y*ᵉ: [inferior bracket not closed]
24–25   ⌊*my faythfull virgins*⌋

Persons

A list of "Persons," evidently an afterthought, appears on page 90v
of the manuscript. It is out of order and omits Mark. Only the following characters receive any description. Sir Gregory is dubbed "a
young rich Country Knight" and Zany "a rich heire." Swallow is
called "a Counsailer and userure." Speak and Plainman are de-
scribed as "two blunt Clownes." Following frequent Restoration
practice we have supplied somewhat fuller descriptions for the convenience of the reader.

Act I

The first page of the text (5r) is seriously stained and is only partially legible. A nineteenth-century transcription signed "A.G." was
found with the manuscript. At several points the transcriber demon-
strably added or misread words, and he seriously distorts the sense
of Rightwit's second speech. His reconstruction follows:

Act the first
      Enter Rightwitt and
      Leonora his sister
Leo[a] You weare never Vertious—
Rightw[t] Practice what thou wilt, not talke of
      Vertue & bee an Asse;—Vertue!
      A thing no one so much as thincks of
      nowe in this age, which is wise, and
      more oute of fashion than a french
      whoad [in margin: "hood?"]; and put on only by some
      moaded [in margin: "modish?"] piteous soules; that are not
      fitt for any thing but to count Aves
      on their beads to keepe themselves
      from sleeping.
Leo[a] You are a precious gallant.
Rightw[t] You are a precious little fool—
      Oh those Eyes of thine!
      Why shouldst thou set free their
      Stormes thus; and round about their
      glorious sunne, Enslave
      those taking refuge from a flame

What we can now read with certainty is as follows:
Act the first
      Enter Rightwitt and
      Leonora his sister
Lea[n] you weare never vertious—
Rig[h] why, what thou wilt not talke of
      vertue and bee an Ass;
      ,a thing no one soe much as thincks
      one in this age that is wise,
      more oute of fashion than a french
      Whood; and put on [blot] only by some old
      moaded pittious soule's; that are not
      fitt for any thing; but to count Ave's
      on their beads to keepe themselves
      from sleeping.
Lea[n] you are a precious gallant.
Right. you are a precious foole
      oh those eyes of thine!

why shouldst thou Let ther [word missing]
stormes thus; and about their [one or more words missing]
glorious sunne [three or more words missing]
those taking Light [word missing] carry
flame

We have supplied appropriate connectives and recorded them
below.

11   cast a pall; [supplied by editors]
11   might [supplied by editors]
12   furious [The MS appears to read *ferriess*, but this word must be
　　　regarded as doubtful.]
18   *scan* is written above *sean*, but the latter is not canceled
20   ǀ*Sir William meanwell*ǀ
25   At least four words are canceled at the end of this speech; the
　　　first three appear to be *I have taryd*
26   *Home What? all*
30   ǀ*nell*ǀ
33   A word, possibly *bastards* is canceled, with *children* careted
　　　above it.
42   *and and Run*
73   ǀ*madam*ǀ
84   *great* is supplied from the catchword
91   *the doe*
96   *servitiure* is careted above *Seruant* (not canceled)
99   illegible word scribbled out after *she is*
100 *she is most perfict in* partially cropped by the binder; *perfict*
　　　has been rewritten (apparently in the same hand) below the
　　　line with a caret
111 *in* written twice with the first one canceled
118 *let* careted and canceled after *please*; *let* careted after *to*
129 scribal blot after *page*
129 *at door*
146 *allamoade* miswritten and canceled
157 speech misassigned to Courtall
159 speech misassigned to Courtall
161–62 *which* canceled before *makes*; *Tis that* careted before
　　　makes
175 *rouge* canceled after *sawcy*
201 ǀ*Well m^r: Zany*ǀ
225 ,ǀ*be not ofended sir*ǀ

226   scribal blot after *is*
243   scribal blot before *rare*
258   ₍*Lord sir*₎

Act II

0.1   Act the Second [written at the top of 15r, though the entrance
        and first four speeches of the act appear on the bottom of 14v,
        under a heavy double line]
37   sparkling [The MS reads *sparcking* with a peculiarly mal-
        formed letter careted above the *i*. Comparison with a careted *l*
        in *talke* on 17r suggests that *sparkling* is intended.]
63   *rascal, gulls*
72–73 *Audience Audience* [word repeated: in the first instance it
        degenerates into a scribble]
73   ₍M*ʳˢ*₎
80   ₍*marck*₎
85   *my* canceled before *masters*
90   *ty dogg*
101   *ane* [e canceled] *Emp$\overline{a}$roll—*
106   *con gree;*
114   bears [supplied from catchword]
120   two illegible letters canceled before *both*
126   *letchery*
128   *are* canceled after *where*
142   ₍*mistriss*₎
143   *ballial* canceled after *son of*
144   *As* canceled after *nothing*
153   *is an a new* [*a* written above the line, without a caret]
155   *preety* written as catchword and scribbled out
159   *hau* canceled before *care*
163   ₍*ye coxcomb*₎
191   *yoel* canceled before *you'l*
194   *y* canceled after *forgett*
196   *am$\overline{oo}$r's*
210   *tres homble Serviteùr mon seigniour seigneure*
215   *sure* miswritten and canceled after *me*; it is rewritten correctly
        below the line.
218   two illegible letters canceled after *but*
252   manuscript reads *mountla*
253   *G* canceled before *to Court*

257   the gilt [The writer wrote *thee Giult* and altered it to *thy Giult.*]
262 |*dear myne*|
262   *at dore*
265   illegible word canceled before *in the*
267   *Extend* canceled after *vast*
270   a word, probably *blast*, canceled before *poyson*
292   *wondrous* canceled, with *horible* written above it
294   *wife wife*
322 |*and use one of these puppies*|
322 |*kindly*|
332   illegible word canceled before *choose*
333   *please* canceled before *will*
336 |*what the plague would you be at* [inferior bracket not closed]
348 |*mistris*|
350   *of* canceled before *oa'fe*
355   speech assigned to "Boy"
357   speech assigned to "Boy"
381–82 |*non abstant*ᵉ|
382   illegible word canceled between *ile* and *doe*
384   *wee'le* canceled with *'twill* written above it
385.1   *Musick*
398–99   *I doe not looke off, every man.* [We have emended to make sense of the passage.]
401   *the dart*
402   *and* canceled with *but* careted above it before *by your*
402   *langug* canceled after *by your*
405 |*madam*|
411–12 |*sweet makelove*|
418   *till I see you.*
421   *the* smeared and canceled before *thee*
423   *when first I see mʳ: Meanwell*
430   *pastm̄e pastime* [first word not canceled; second careted above it]
435   *Ere* canceled with *nea'r* careted above it
443   *I can scare forbear*
458 |*Sweet myne*|
460 |*my dear*|
462   illegible words canceled after *shall*
462   He brings [*He* has been supplied by the editors.]
463 |*ralph*|

475   *noe* canceled before *none*

476.1   illegible word canceled after *weepe*

481   *to* overinked and canceled before *too*

486   ₗ*we all waytte* [inferior bracket not closed]

488   *these two days* canceled after *where have you been?*

492–93   MS appears to read *had I tript afaire that distemper* [We have emended to make sense of the passage.]

506   besides [supplied from catchword]

507   *me* written above a smeared attempt to write *me*, without a caret

517   three or four illegible letters canceled before *indignation*

521   ₗ*S*ʳ:ₗ

522   *him* canceled before *and turne*

534   *good* canceled after *your*

540   *ruining* [written twice and canceled in the first instance]

551   *desigie* canceled before *designe*

557–58   *If Love . . . night* [not lineated as a couplet in the MS]

565   illegible word canceled after *would*

575   ₗ*for her*ₗ

579   *but* canceled before *yet*

585   *ye* cancelled before *sute's*, with *the* written above it [A *y* has been added to *the*, possibly in another hand; *the* for *they* is a mistake which occurs several times in this MS.]

587–88   *Please . . . win* [not lineated as a couplet in the MS]

Act III

0.1   *the third Act.*

16   *must* written above *will* [canceled]

22   *doe* canceled before *tells*

30   *the begin*

36   *the shall*

53   illegible letter canceled before *your*

58   *s* canceled at the end of *Come*

65   *how old is the* canceled; *what tyme of* careted before *night*

66–67   *old Ruffian, Home* [We have added *should go* to make sense of the passage.]

84   *the doe*

90   *wenche's* canceled after *wine nor*

128   *off* canceled after *watching*, with *ffor* written above it, and the *or* canceled; *for* careted before *your*

128   *so* canceled before *that he*

133   *her* canceled before *usage*
136.1   *the play*
150   *aloon, aloon,*
160   of [supplied from catchword]
172   *vll* canceled before *vilanous*
176   *of* canceled after *cloaths*
182   *verry* canceled; *Mon'st'rous* written above it without a caret
196   two illegible letters canceled before *acting*
201–203   *Lets . . . pay.* [not lineated as a couplet in the MS]
203   two illegible words canceled before *rascall* with *the* careted
          above them
203   The last line on page 49v, partially cropped by the binder, has
          been rewritten above it.

Act IV
0.1   *the fourth Act.*
0.2   *playne*
5   *where* canceled before *a pox*
6–7   ₁*m* *Rightw.*ᵗ*ₜ*₁
28.1   *marke the Constable*
28.2–28.3   *Habitt.*
41   *strange* canceled after *old*
46   *profess* [*I* supplied by editors]
52   *chilld little.*
58   ₁*Sir*₁
59   behold [supplied from catchword]
69   *are* canceled; *were* written above it, with no caret
69   ₁*from whence*₁
72   withdraw [written twice, with the first one canceled]
87   *the* canceled before *and every thing*
97   ₁*mʳ: Meanwell*₁
106   *to* canceled before *upont*
118   ₁*sweet*₁
122   ₁*my man*₁
125   ₁*Come*₁
129.1   *the pull*
150   ₁*what*₁
178   *you* canceled after *amiss*
185   ₁*Sʳ:*₁
186.1   *the tye*
190   illegible word canceled after *and*, with *Be sure* careted above it

206   *away another word away upon thee* [second *away* careted]
207   *shall* canceled after *rayling—it*
213   *agen* canceled after *loaded*
216   *not* canceled after *aske me*
216.1   *unbinds him* [We have added PHILARIO for clarity.]
224   *att distance*
229   Fear . . . fear [The text appears corrupt here. The last line of
        61v reads *fear nothing. it Comes*; the catchword, *with,* is duly
        picked up at the top of 62r, which reads *with a fear.* Probably
        the author's eye jumped to a *with* farther down the page.]
234 |*mark*|
238   illegible word canceled before *but hange*
241 |*lord*|
245   him [supplied from catchword]
246 |*bones*|
247 |*seem's*|
249–50 |*nurses sirha*|
250   *whis* canceled before *whilst*
252 |*mark*|
257 |*M$^{rs:}$*|
260   *oh mounsiure playne—tr'es homble servaunt.*
261 |*in fayth*|
271–72   cutting a purse, man? [The MS originally read *cutting a
        purss.* The word *man* with a terminal period was written in
        later at the end of the line in lighter ink.]
290   *that* canceled after *pitty;*
296 |*you sure mistake my lord*|
303 |*worthy Sir frances*|
305   *has* canceled before *ha's money*
307–308   *And . . . woo* [not lineated as a couplet in the MS]
308   *I* canceled before *I for*
308.1   *Marke Clarabell*
318 |*marke*|
318   *need's* canceled before *neede's see*
328.2   and Speak [supplied by editors]
336   *Faith . . . almost* [line partially cropped by binder]
342 |*I hope Sir*|
348   *how* canceled before *how like*
352   illegible word canceled after *leggs*
358ff.   [The lineation of the songs follows the rhyme scheme
        rather than the MS lineation.]

360   *then* [written twice, with the second one canceled]
360   *thinck* canceled before *thickness*
362   *qu* canceled before *Cure*
376   *and his* canceled with *their* careted above it before *fortune*
377   *Certayne* canceled before *graunted*
380   *Courag^e* canceled after *youth and*
390–91   *occasion . . . master.* [There is a hiatus in the MS at this point. The last line of page 69v has been almost totally cropped and is unrecoverable. The top line of 70r has been partially cropped, but is legible, except the first word. Since the accidental conjunction of "occasion" and "with her master" makes sense, we have not ventured a conjectural reconstruction.]
406   *hange me;* canceled before *Contemn mee*
431   money to pay [*to pay* was written twice, with *pay* as the catchword at the bottom of 71v]
436   *Aloun*
437   open, in [These words are separated by a page break, 72r–72v. The last word at the bottom of 72r is *to,* evidently an error.]
440.2   *phlario marke—*
448   *I have it* canceled; *thou hast it* written above it with no caret
448   *All laugh* [This stage direction is partially cropped at the bottom of 72v, and our reading cannot be considered certain.]
449   [Two words are canceled at the beginning of this speech. The first is *I'm.* The second is illegible. The writer was in a muddle, since the speech tag, correctly anticipated in the catchword at the bottom of the preceding page, does not come until after the cancellation.]
464   *Clar^b. mark.*

Act V

0.1   *Act fifth*
4   words [supplied by the editors. The top line of page 74r is wavering and partly cropped. One word is completely lost.]
12   [*in Ernest*]
15–16   her, though my fortune never can [Part of the top line of page 74v is cropped and unrecoverable. We can read *my fortune never Can* and we can take the first word, *her,* from the catchword on 74r. We have added *though* as a plausible connective. The missing word does appear to have contained a *g* near the end.]

20   *there has*

26   two illegible letters have been canceled after *Embrace you*

28   *against you.* [The *you* has been supplied in a nineteenth-
      century hand and ink below the line; the original was evi-
      dently cropped by the binder.]

35   two illegible words canceled after *acquainted with*; *itt* is writ-
      ten above them, with no caret

52–53   *near* canceled before *him*, with *at* careted above it

60   *af* canceled before *efected*

64   *to carry ye* [written in at the beginning of a line in the left
      margin]

65 |*clear as the day*|

77 |*and marke*|

82.1–82.2   *procreate m^{rs}: fayth:*

88 |*marry M^{rs} fayth*|

95   *the* canceled before *business*; *your* written above it with no
      caret

96 |*is my Cosen*|

98   *deser* canceled before *meritt's*

100 |*bawding*|

100   *in* [written twice and canceled in the first instance]

103 |*soe please*|

113 |*now if you*| *cosen fayth*|

115   illegible letter canceled before *dance*

123   *seaven* canceled after *just*; *six* written above it with no caret

125   *Country* canceled before *love*; *chosen* written above it with no
      caret

126 |*you for another madam*|

130 |*cosen rightwitt*|

130   *that* canceled after *fortune*; *to have* written above it with no
      caret

138   *conjurer* [written twice and canceled in the first instance]

139   *to* canceled before *nothing*

143   *Ele's* canceled after *me*

143–44   illegible word canceled after *every where*; *thus* careted
      above it

144 |*I must speake to him*|

146–47 |*that Codshead Zany*|

150   *fa* canceled before *jewell*

152   *wher* canceled before *out of*

155 *out* overinked after *find* and written again careted above the line, possibly in a different hand
157 *Id* canceled before *I would*
177 a word, probably *foole,* canceled before *knight*
179 |*Sir*|
190 |*dear meanwell*|
193 |*sir william*|
204 |*Madam*|
209 |*soe chayre men*|
209 *d* canceled before *dore*
210 *Exitt Sed* [Word cropped; we have added *carriers.*]
216 *The sedan did indeed* [This line is written twice at the top of page 83v, with the first instance scribbled out.]
220 *E* cancelled after *they come*
227.1 *procreat leanora*
231 *the will*
237.2 *went* canceled before *out*; *danct* written above it with no caret
237.3 *Makelove pulls . . .* [The bracketed passage has been supplied by the editors. The last part of the stage direction has been cropped, but the sense is obvious.]
238 |*brother Meanwell* [inferior bracket not closed]
240–41 *a* canceled before *good,* with *the* written above it with no caret
250 |*m^r: Zany*|
251 daughter [The MS reads *dayhte* with the end of the word cropped.]
260 *heres is*
261 *righte* canceled before *bride*
261 |*myne*|
273 |*lawyer*|
276 *intere* canceled after *cutt of his*
280 *the* [written twice and canceled in the second instance]
281 *y* canceled before *his futer*
283 |*by marriage*|
293 *as ye* canceled after *pasion*
301 *unt* canceled after *leave his*
305 |*Sirha: ralph*|
311 *wife* canceled after *from my,* with *lady* careted above it
313 |*Sir pray be gon*|

315   *kave* canceled before *knave's*
317 |*is vayne*|
320 |*by an old proverbe*|
323   *man*
324   of chosen nation [words supplied by editors to fit rhyme scheme in place of an illegible scribble]
341   illegible scribble after *once*

THE FROLICKS

Designed by R. E. Rosenbaum.
Composed by Vail-Ballou Press, Inc.,
in 10 point VIP Primer, 2 points leaded,
with display lines in Primer.
Printed offset by Vail-Ballou Press on
Warren's No. 66 text, 50 pound basis.
Bound by Vail-Ballou Press
in Joanna book cloth
and stamped in All Purpose foil.

Library of Congress Cataloging in Publication Data
(For library cataloging purposes only)

Polwhele, Elizabeth.
  The frolicks, or the lawyer cheated (1671)

  I. Title.
PR3619.P67F7   1977   822'.4   77-3125
ISBN 0-8014-1030-4